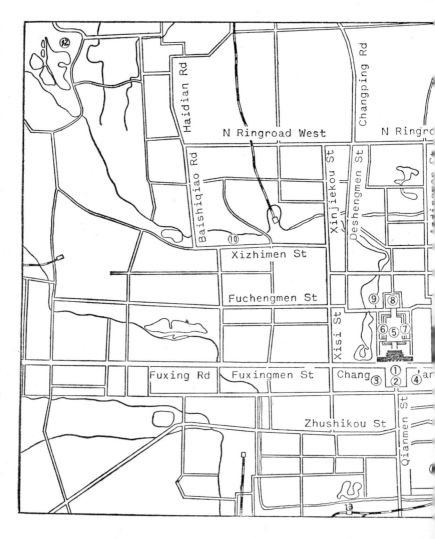

G

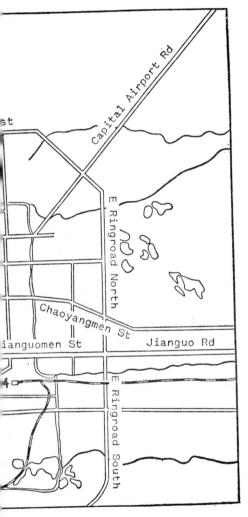

1 Monument to the
  People's Heroes
2 Chairman Mao Zedong
  Memorial Hall
3 Great Hall of
  the People
4 Museum of the Chinese
  Revolution and Museum
  of Chinese History
5 Palace Museum
6 Zhongshan Park
7 The Working People's
  Palace of Culture
8 Jingshan Park
9 Beihai Park
10 Beijing Zoo
11 Tiantan Park
12 Yiheyuan (Summer
   Palace)
13 Yongdingmen Railway
   Station
14 Beijing Railway
   Station

BEIJING

China's Ancient and Modern Capital

Liu Junwen

Foreign Languages Press   Beijing

First Edition   1982
Second Edition   1991

ISBN 0-8351-2408-8
ISBN 7-119-01221-5

Published by Foreign Languages Press
24 Baiwanzhuang Road, Beijing 100037, China

Printed by Foreign Languages Printing House
19 Chegongzhuang Xilu, Beijing 100044, China

Distributed by China International Book Trading Corporation
21 Chegongzhuang Xilu, Beijing 100044, China
P.O. Box 399, Beijing, China

Printed in the People's Republic of China

Contents

1

Beijing:[1] A City in Change

Beijing is a modern city with roots stretching far back into remote antiquity. During the course of its history it has played various roles, been known by different names and changed its boundaries many times. To appreciate the fascination that this city has exerted on many generations of residents and visitors we must know a little of its history: its transformation from prehistoric village to thriving metropolis, from imperial capital to the capital of the People's Republic of China.

The Early Beginnings

According to historians and geologists, the area around modern Beijing was a gulf two or three million years ago, semi-enclosed by the Taihang Mountains to the west and the Yanshan Mountains to the north. The melting ice and snow and the heavy rains carried enormous amounts of mud and silt down from the mountain valleys into the gulf. Years of accumulation transformed the gulf into an alluvial plain known today as the Beijing Sub-plain.

The Beijing Sub-plain forms the northern apex of the vast North China Plain and is protected from the

[1]北京。

1

severe cold of the north by mountains to the north, west and southwest. Some 140 kilometres to the southeast lies the Gulf of Bohai which affords some degree of moisture from the sea. The mild climate and plentiful rainfall favour the growth of vegetation and perhaps explain why Beijing became a human settlement at a very early stage. However, the uncertainty of summer rains due to its continental climate often brings drought to this area.

The earliest inhabitant of the Beijing Sub-plain that we know of today was Peking Man, a primitive caveman who lived about 500,000 years ago at Dragon Bone Hill by the town of Zhoukoudian,[1] southwest of Beijing. The Peking Man caves are still in a good state of preservation and provide a popular historic site for visitors.

Early Townships on the Guang'anmen Site

Many thousands of years later, about one or two thousand years BC, some small settlements began to appear on the Beijing Sub-plain. One of them was located around the present Guang'anmen (Gate of Vast Peace) area in southwestern Beijing. The Guang'anmen settlement lay in the path a natural corridor connecting the Yellow River valley to the south with the Songliao Plain to the northeast and Mongolian Plateau to the north. There is evidence of an early ferry crossing over the Yongding River south of Beijing at Lugouqiao, not far from Zhoukoudian. The Guang'anmen settlement thus became a centre of north-south communications. With the development of production and increase in commerce in the Zhou dynasty, it grew into a prosperous market

---

[1]周口店。

town. Ji[1] or Jicheng[2] (Thistle Town), as it was called, was the earliest predecessor of Beijing.

In the 11th century BC the northern kingdom of Yan[3] became a powerful independent state. Its capital was at Jicheng, which also became known as Yanjing[4] (Yan Capital). Jicheng continued as the capital of Yan for eight or nine hundred years, and was an important metropolis in north China. In 221 BC, Qin Shihuang,[5] the First Emperor of the Qin dynasty, conquered the other six kingdoms in central and north China and established a unified centralized state with its capital at Xianyang[6] (in present-day Shaanxi). The state of Yan ceased to exist and Jicheng became an ordinary prefectural town. However it still remained as a major trading centre and a place of strategic importance.

During the Tang dynasty (618-907), Jicheng was renamed Youzhou[7] (Remote Prefecture). It was from here that the rebellion led by An Lushan[8] and Shi Siming[9] was launched in 755, presenting a grave threat to the continuation of Tang rule. From Youzhou the rebels fought their way to Chang'an,[10] the Tang capital, and occupied it. A stone stele erected by Shi Siming is still preserved in the Fayuansi (Temple of the Source of the Law) in Beijing. The An-Shi rebellion was crushed a few years later, but the golden age of the Tang empire had already passed and again unified China split up into several states.

Capital of the Northern Dynasties

In the 10th century the Tang was succeeded by the

[1]蓟；[2]蓟城；[3]燕；[4]燕京；[5]秦始皇；[6]咸阳；[7]幽州；[8]安禄山；[9]史思明；[10]长安。

Song dynasty in central and south China and by the Liao dynasty in the north. The Qidan[1] (Khitan), a Mongolian tribe from the West Liao River area in north China, founded the Liao dynasty in 947. In 936 it occupied Youzhou and designated it a secondary capital of the Liao, named Nanjing[2] (Southern Capital). The older name, Yanjing, came into use again in the 11th century although the Liao continued to hold it until 1122.

Remains of the Liao dynasty can still be found in Beijing. The Tianningsi (Temple of Heavenly Tranquillity) pagoda near Guang'anmen is an elaborately constructed building from the Liao dynasty, and a Liao stele recording the erection of a magnificent tower to house the Buddhist Tripitaka is preserved in the Dajuesi (Temple of Great Awakening) in the Western Hills.

In the 12th century the Nüzhen[3] (Jurchen), a Tungusic tribe from the Songhua River in the northeast, drove out the Qidan and set up the Jin dynasty. Pushing south they occupied Yanjing in 1122 and thence extended their influence as far as the northern borders of the Qinling Mountains and the Huai River in central China. In order to maintain control over the Yellow River valley and at the same time remain in easy contact with their base in the northeast, the Nüzhen established their main capital at Yanjing and named it Zhongdu[4] (Central Capital). Zhongdu thus became the centre of rule over half of China.

Extensive rebuilding was carried out in Zhongdu under the Jin. The old city borders to the east, south and west were enlarged and a new imperial palace was erected in the centre of the town. The new palace was very grand, modelled after the imperial palace at Bian-

[1]契丹；[2]南京；[3]女真；[4]中都。

liang,[1] capital of the Northern Song dynasty (present-day Kaifeng).

The most splendid legacy bequeathed to Beijing by the Jin is Lugouqiao[2] (known to the West as the Marco Polo Bridge), spanning the Yongding River. The old ferry crossing at this site, which has served since ancient times as a gateway to Beijing from the Yellow River valley, had been replaced by a wooden pontoon bridge which could be easily washed away or burnt down. To meet the military, political, economic and cultural needs of the new imperial capital, the Jin emperor ordered the construction of a great stone bridge there in 1189.

Lugouqiao is a remarkable engineering feat. Built almost eight centuries ago, it can still bear a load of more than four hundred tons without a tremor. Even more remarkable is its appearance. Along each side is a marble balustrade with altogether two hundred and eighty balusters, and on each bluster is a large stone lion, some with one or two smaller ones around it, no two of which are alike. Today the bridge is a world famous tourist attraction. To the Chinese people it has an additional significance: it was here that popular armed resistance to Japanese aggression flared up on 7 July 1937, marking the beginning of the War of Resistance Against Japan (1937-45).

Also dating from the Jin is a group of Buddhist pagodas at the foot of the Iron Wall Silver Hill in Changping,[3] north of Beijing. These ancient buildings in their rural setting are particularly attractive in autumn, against the background of the hills and the clear blue sky.

[1]汴梁；[2]芦沟桥；[3]昌平。

The Resiting of the Capital

The early 13th century saw the Mongolians in the
north rapidly gathering strength. In 1215 a cavalry force
under Genghis Khan broke through the natural barrier
at Nankou[1] (Southern Entry) south of the Great Wall and
captured Zhongdu. During the fighting, this magnificent
city, less than a hundred years old, was razed to the
ground.

Fired with the ambition of bringing all of China
under one rule, Kublai Khan, grandson of Genghis, came
down to Zhongdu from the Mongolian steppes in 1260.
He decided to rebuild the old city as a centre from which
to extend his rule over the whole country. The new
capital was named Khanbaliq (Khan's Town) and was
known in Chinese as Dadu[2] (Great Capital).

When Kublai entered Zhongdu, the only palace
which had escaped destruction was the relatively iso-
lated Daninggong (Palace of Great Tranquillity) in the
northeast suburbs outside the Jin city. It was here that
Kublai settled and made the centre of Dadu, roughly
where Beihai (North Lake) Park stands today.

The construction of Dadu opened a new chapter in
the history of Beijing. From its earliest beginnings to
the establishment of Zhongdu as the capital of half of
China, the centre of the city had been in the area around
present-day Guang'anmen. From the rebuilding of Dadu
to the present, the centre has remained where Kublai
decreed his new capital. It was here that Kublai founded
the Yuan dynasty in 1271 after the defeat of the Southern
Song, bringing north and south China again under one
rule. Dadu became the national capital, a position which

[1]南口; [2]大都。

it maintained under different names and in different dynasties down to the present with only minor interruptions.

The construction of Dadu was carried out according to a comprehensive plan. In the centre and to the south was the Imperial City, which consisted of three groups of palaces standing on the banks of Zhonghai (Central Lake) and Beihai. The palaces on the east bank, where the Yuan emperor gave audience and had his residence, were known as Danei[1] (Great Within), the predecessor of the Ming and Qing "Forbidden City". The southern and northern palaces on the west banks of the lakes were the residences of the crown prince and the empress dowager. The palace roofs were resplendent with brightly coloured glazed tiles, the terraces were of intricately carved white marble and the interiors were lavishly decorated.

In the centre of the city, north of the palace, stood the Drum Tower and behind it was the Bell Tower, where drums and bells were beaten to mark the hours of the day and night.

The wall surrounding the city had two gates to the north and three gates on each of the other three sides. Broad, straight roads ran between opposite pairs of gates, and it was said that someone standing at one end of the road could see the other end. Apart from these broad avenues, the principal streets mostly ran north-south, intersected by *hutong* (lanes) running east-west. Some of the principal streets and lanes still exist: Dongdan Street, Xidan Street, Dongsi Street, Xisi Street, Dongzhimen Road, Xizhimen Road, Gulou West Road and Inner Chaoyangmen Road all existed in Dadu under different names.

[1] 大内。

Neither a river nor coastal city, Dadu was handi-
capped by a limited water supply, and Kublai commis-
sioned the famous hydraulic engineer Guo Shoujing[1] to
overcome the problem. Guo first improved the supply
of drinking water by bringing the waters of the Jade
Spring in the Western Hills into the city at Jishuitan[2]
(Water Accumulating Pool) near present Deshengmen
(Gate of Victory) in northwest Beijing. He later built
the Tonghui Canal, linking Tongzhou (now Tongxian),
the terminal of the Grand Canal, with Jishuitan. The
Tonghui extension, opened in 1293, enabled canal barges
from the south to enter the city. The area between Jishuitan and the Drum Tower thus became the commercial centre of the city.

The prosperous city of Dadu attracted many foreign traders and monks, and the frequent contacts between Yuan China and foreign countries promoted the
growth of cultural exchange. The Baitasi (Temple of
the White Pagoda), which still stands inside Fuchengmen
today, was rebuilt with the help of a Nepalese named
Arnico. Marco Polo, who was deeply impressed by the
grandeur of the city and its palaces, claimed that no
other city in the world could rival it; a detailed descrip-
tion of "Cambaluc" is given in his account of his travels.

Beijing Under the Ming

In the mid-14th century, Zhu Yuanzhang[3] led a successful rebellion against the Yuan in central China, and
founded the Ming dynasty in 1368 with its capital at
present-day Nanjing[4] (Nanking). In the same year his
general Xu Da[5] launched a northern expedition against

[1]郭守敬；[2]积水潭；[3]朱元璋；[4]南京；[5]徐达。

the last Yuan emperor in Dadu, who fled back to the Mongolian steppes. Xu Da captured Dadu and renamed it Beiping (Northern Peace). He also reduced the size of the city by moving its northern wall south to its present location along the line marked by Deshengmen and Andingmen (Gate of Stability). The ruins of the Yuan northern wall can still be seen today beyond Deshengmen, an earthen mound rather grandly known as the "Earthen Wall". There used to be a scenic spot here known as "Trees in the Mist at the Ji Gate", one of the "Eight Sights of Yanjing", but today all that remains is the stele on an earthen mound northeast of Deshengmen bearing this name.

One of Zhu Yuanzhang's sons, Zhu Di, was made prince of Yan and given Beiping as his domain. In 1403, Zhu Di became the third Ming emperor, adopting the reign title Yongle. In 1421 he formally transferred the court to Beiping and renamed the city Beijing (Northern Capital), the name it retains today.

The Yongle emperor rebuilt Beijing on the foundations of Dadu, drawing on earlier Chinese capitals, especially Nanjing, for inspiration. Among the achievements of his reign are the Forbidden City, imperial residences and halls, altars, temples, and the Drum and Bell towers. A wall more than twenty kilometres long enclosed the city, to which were later added nine great towers.

When rebuilding was completed, Beijing was much larger than Dadu, and its outlines were very different. The northern city wall was much further south, and the southern city wall was also carried south from its Yuan boundary along present-day Chang'an Avenue to the east-west line marked by the present Qianmen (Front Gate). The southern walls of the Imperial City and the Forbidden

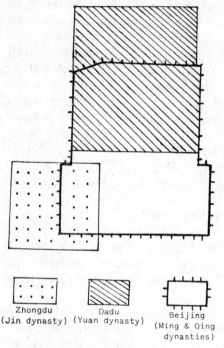

Zhongdu
(Jin dynasty)

Dadu
(Yuan dynasty)

Beijing
(Ming & Qing
dynasties)

CHANGES IN THE SITE OF BEIJING

City were also brought further south. During the reign of the Jiajing emperor (1522-1566) another city wall was added enclosing the southern suburbs. Beijing then became a "double town", with a square "inner city" and an oblong "outer city" to the south. This layout remained unchanged until the liberation of Beijing in 1949.

The palaces in the Forbidden City, which are now open to the public, were built and occupied by the Yongle emperor. Its main buildings lie along a north-south central axis about eight kilometres long which passes through the entire city, from Yongdingmen (Gate of Eternal Pacification) in the south to the Bell and Drum towers in the north. Going north from Yongdingmen along this axis are Zhengyangmen, popularly known as Qianmen, the entrance to the Imperial City; Tiananmen (Gate of Heavenly Peace) and Duanmen (Gate of Correct Demeanour); Wumen (Meridian Gate), the entrance

to the Forbidden City; Taihemen (Gate of Supreme Harmony), and the three front palaces; the three rear
palaces; the Imperial Garden; Shenwumen (Gate of
Divine Might), the northern entrance to the Forbidden
City; and the central peak of Jingshan (Prospect Hill),
also known as Meishan (Coal Hill), at the rear of the
Imperial City. Other important buildings flanking the
central axis are the Taimiao (Supreme Ancestral Temple),
now the Workers' Cultural Palace, and the Shejitan
(Altar of Land and Grain), now Zhongshan Park, to the
east and west respectively of Tiananmen, and Tiantan
(Altar of Heaven), now a public park, and Xiannongtan
(Altar of the Creator of Agriculture), now a sports field,
on either side of Yongdingmen.

The Great Wall of China, perhaps China's most famous ancient relic, stands at one point not far north
of Beijing. This section of the wall, which winds in a
general northwest direction for about twenty kilometres,
was rebuilt under the Ming as a protection to Beijing
and is now a popular tourist site. At Badaling (Eight
Prominent Peaks) sixty kilometres from Beijing, a small
square fort also dating from the Ming stands in front of
the wall on the Beijing side. The road from Beijing to
Badaling first passes through Nankou and Juyongguan
(Dwelling-in-Harmony Pass) to reach the fort through
which the road leads beyond the wall. The east gate at
the entrance to the fort bears an inscription reading "The
Outpost to Juyong"; on the west gate, which is connected
on both sides to the wall itself, the inscription reads "The
Northern Strategic Gate".

Another famous site north of Beijing is the Ming
Tombs, a burial ground of the Ming emperors, known
to the Chinese as Shisanling (Thirteen Tombs). The

largest is Changling, the tomb of the Yongle emperor. Dingling, the tomb of the fourth last Ming emperor Wanli (1573-1620), is the only one so far excavated. When it was opened in 1956-58, it was discovered that the tomb was as lavishly decorated as the imperial residences; this underground palace cost eight million ounces of silver to build at a time when an ounce of silver could buy 240 kilogrammes of rice.

In 1644 a peasant army led by Li Zicheng[1] captured Beijing and overthrew the Ming empire. Forty-three days later, Manchu forces occupied the city and Beijing became the capital of the Manchu Qing dynasty.

Capital of the Qing

The Qing rulers devoted large amounts of money and manpower into improving or founding new pleasure grounds in and around the city. Improvements were made to the Forbidden City, which they continued to use as the imperial palace, and to Beihai Park within the Imperial City. The Tibetan-style Baita (White Dagoba) in Beihai Park was built at this time.

One of the greatest achievements of the Qing is a vast complex of imperial gardens and palaces laid out in the Kangxi (1662-1722) and Qianlong (1736-95) reigns on the northwestern outskirts of Beijing, known collectively as the summer palaces. The most famous of these is the Yiheyuan[2] (Park of Nurtured Harmony), which is furthest towards the Western Hills. Palaces and gardens have existed on this site since the Jin dynasty. In 1750, Wengshanpo (Jar Hill Pond) was enlarged and renamed Kunming Lake, and Wengshan (Jar

[1]李自成；[2]颐和园。

Hill) was renamed Wanshoushan (Longevity Hill); the whole area was enclosed by a wall and called the Qingyi-yuan[1] (Park of Clear Ripples). In 1860, an Anglo-French joint force invaded Beijing and sacked the Qing-yiyuan. Later the Empress Dowager Cixi[2] used the taxes raised to build a modern Chinese navy to restore and improve the park in 1888, and renamed it the Yi-heyuan. Generally known in English as the Summer Palace, it is a popular spot with visitors the year round.

Not far from the Yiheyuan are the ruins of the old summer palace known as the Yuanmingyuan[3] (Park of Perfection and Brightness). There are altogether three separate parks on this site: the Yuanmingyuan proper, Changchunyuan[4] (Park of Everlasting Spring) and Wan-chunyuan[5] (Park of Ten Thousand Springs), occupying altogether an area of 3,000 hectares. The parks boasted more than a hundred beauty spots and were also the re-pository of valuable books and art treasures. In the north-ern part of Changchunyuan were a set of palaces in the European style, built between 1740 and 1747 in con-sultation with Jesuit priests. In 1860, this "Garden of Gardens" as it was known in the West was sacked by the Anglo-French joint force. All the wooden Chinese buildings were destroyed and only a few ruins of the European palaces remained. Some of the remaining treas-ures were housed in the new Summer Palace or else-where, and the rest gradually disappeared as the site was abandoned. Today its lakes are mainly rice paddies, and small villages occupy part of the grounds. A project for its restoration is now underway.

Apart from the imperial parks, gardens on a smaller

[1]清漪园；[2]慈禧；[3]圆明园；[4]长春园；[5]万春园。

scale were owned by high officials and noble families, but today very few of these private gardens remain.

Modern Beijing

After the Opium War of 1840 China became a semi-colonial and semi-feudal society. Like the country as a whole, Beijing struggled along with a feeble economy and its people living in misery. But the Chinese people refused to be slaves, and waged an unremitting war against the ruling class and foreign imperialism. The May 4th Movement of 1919, which started in Beijing, heralded the New Democratic Revolution in China. It was also in Beijing that the revolutionary martyr Li Dazhao[1] first disseminated Marxism, and in Beijing that the great writer and thinker Lu Xun[2] fought the enemy with his pen. Ancient Beijing became the birthplace of revolution in modern China.

On October 1, 1949, on the rostrum above Tiananmen, Mao Zedong[3] declared the founding of the People's Republic of China: "The Chinese people have stood up!" This opened a new chapter in the history of Beijing.

As the capital of the People's Republic, Beijing is the centre of political life for people of all ethnic groups in China. The National People's Congresses and the congresses of the Chinese Communist Party are held here, as are many other important conferences. Beijing is also the country's scientific and cultural centre, where China's scientists, scholars, artists and technicians, along with workers and peasants, are making their contribution to China's modernization.

[1]李大钊；[2]鲁迅；[3]毛泽东。

2

Tiananmen and Tiananmen Square

Located in the heart of Beijing, Tiananmen (Gate of Heavenly Peace) stands in front of the entrance to the former Imperial Palace facing Tiananmen Square. Between the gate and the square is Chang-an Avenue running from east to west. To the east, south and west are the city's busiest commercial districts — Wangfujing, Dazhalan and Xidan. Pedestrian and other traffic converge here from all directions. It is the starting point for visits to the Imperial Palace, the Chairman Mao Zedong Memorial Hall, the Great Hall of the People, the Museum of Chinese History, the Museum of the Chinese Revolution, and the Monument to the People's Heroes.

Tiananmen Gate-tower, the Marble Bridges and Carved Ornamental Columns

Tiananmen was first erected in 1420 after the establishment of Beijing as the capital of China in the Ming dynasty, and was first known as Chengtianmen (Gate for Receiving Orders from the Heaven). Seriously damaged during the fighting at the end of the Ming, it was rebuilt under the Qing in 1651 and given its present name. During the Ming and Qing dynasties, it was the south and main gate to the Imperial City, the residential and administrative quarters of court officials and retainers who served the Imperial Palace. The red south wall of the old Imperial City, with its yellow glazed-tile roof, still reaches along either side of Tiananmen. The gate itself consists of a red platform with five vaulted gateways, surmounted by a wooden gate-tower. The top of the platform provides a rostrum for viewing the square in front.

The gate-tower has a double roof of yellow glazed tiles and vermilion columns. The roof is in *xieshan* style, a traditional style of Chinese palace architecture, fully hipped on two sides, and half-hipped at the ends so that an upper gable is left exposed. The four side ridges lead to overhanging corner eaves supported by elaborate bracketing. The ridges of the upper roof are decorated with altogether ten glazed tile *wenshou* (zoomorphic figures): a pair of dragon-headed figures (*zhengwen*) are perched at each end of the central ridge and two *wenshou* stand on each of the four side ridges. These figures have tails like a kind of owl called in Chinese "cathead eagle". According to legend, there is a kind of fish-dragon in the southern sea which has a tail like the "cathead eagle", and this tail can stir up the waves to make rain. It was formerly believed that placing *wenshou* with their "cathead eagle" tails on roof ridges could prevent fire. On the backs of the *zhengwen* at the ends of the main ridge are two fan-shaped swords, which are supposed to prevent them escaping. Apart from the *wenshou*, there are ten other figures on the ridges: an immortal, dragon, phoenix, lion, *qilin* (mythical beast), sea-horse, sky-horse, fish, *xia* and *hou* (mythical beasts). When the gate-tower was built these figures were placed there to ward off evil and calamity, but today they serve as beautiful ornamentation.

The massive roofs and eaves are supported by regularly placed brackets. The brackets and roof beams are beautifully patterned in scarlet, gold, blue and green. On the southern face of the tower are thirty-six rhomboid-latticed windows, and beneath them runs a colourfully painted skirting board. The tower is nine bays wide and five bays deep: according to ancient records, the combination of the numbers nine and five symbolizes the emperor, and its use by others is strictly forbidden. The platform beneath the tower stands more than ten metres high on a white marble waisted *sumeru* pedestal; it is constructed from large bricks each weighing twenty-four kilogrammes and is painted vermilion. From base to roof top the whole gate-tower measures 33.7 metres.

Tiananmen was also known as the State Portal. The Taimiao (Supreme Ancestral Temple) lay to the east and the Shejitan (Altar of Land and Grain) to the west: the former held the ancestral tablets of the imperial family, while the latter was for holding sacrifices to the Local God of Land. At the time of the winter solstice the Ming and Qing emperors offered annual sacrifices at the Tiantan (Altar of Heaven) in the southern city; at the summer solstice they offered sacrifices at the Ditan (Altar of Earth) in the northern part of the city; and at the beginning of spring they prayed for good harvests at the Temple of the Xiannongtan (Altar of the Creator of Agriculture). On these important occasions, the four main gates to the Imperial Palace were thrown open: Wumen, Duanmen, Tiananmen and Zhonghuamen (Central Flowery Gate; no longer extant). The emperor, dressed in full imperial regalia, passed through at the head of a grand procession of civil and military officials. When the emperor personally led his troops into battle, he made a sacrifice for the journey in front of Tiananmen; when one of his generals set out for battle, the emperor would head a procession of civil and military officials here to offer a sacrifice to the flag. At the end of the year he would also make a sacrifice to the flag here. It was a sacred, solemn place during these two dynasties.

The grandest of all ceremonies held at Tiananmen during the Ming and Qing was the issuing of imperial edicts. First, the Minister of Rites would receive the edict in the Taihedian inside the palace, place it on a "cloud tray", raise above it the imperial yellow umbrella and thus proceed through Taihemen. Then he would put the tray in a miniature "dragon pavilion", which would be carried through Wumen to the stand set up on the Tiananmen gate-tower. There the edict would be proclaimed by an edict-proclaiming official. The civil and military officials of the court, lining up according to rank south of the Outer Gold Water River Bridges, would kneel down facing north towards the emperor. The edict would then be put in the mouth of a gilded wooden phoenix which was lowered by a rope (or, during the Ming, carried in the mouth of a dragon head on top of a pole) to a "cloud tray" held below by an official of the Ministry of Rites. Again it would be put in a miniature "dragon pavilion" and carried to the Ministry of Rites beneath an imperial yellow umbrella. Then the edict would be copied out on yellow paper and sent around the country to be made known to all. This was called "the golden phoenix issues an edict".

The small stream in front of Tiananmen is called the Outer Gold Water River (Wai Jinshuihe), its source being the Gold Water River in Changping in the western outskirts of the city. The upper course of the river, which flows in front of the Gate of Supreme Harmony and forms a moat around the Imperial Palace, is called the Inner Gold Water River. Seven bridges span the Outer Gold Water River. The two at either side used to be called the Gongshengqiao (Public Bridges); they now stand outside Zhongshan Park and the Beijing Working People's Palace of Culture. The five in the middle are generally known in Chinese as the Outer Gold Water Bridges and in English as the Marble Bridges. The bridges are slightly arched and wider at the ends than in the middle, creating a decorative effect that can be best appreciated from the gate-tower.

The bridge in the middle of the five Marble Bridges is larger than the others and was used exclusively by the emperor; it is called the Yuluqiao (Bridge of the Imperial Way). The two bridges on either side were called the Wanggongqiao (Royal Bridges) and were for the use of the imperial relatives. The two outer bridges were called the Pingjiqiao (Ranking Bridges) and were for civil and military officials above the third rank. Those of the fourth rank and below were only allowed to cross the Public Bridges. The five gateways under the gate-tower, called "the Five Passes", were graded the same way; no one except the emperor was allowed to pass through the middle one. This feudal ranking system also finds expression in carvings on the balustrades of the bridges: coiled dragons are carved on the right balusters of the Bridge of the Imperial Way while lotus flowers appear on the balusters of the other bridges.

Before and behind the gateways are two pairs of white marble columns, called *huabiao* (carved ornamental columns). Two stone lions stand in front of the gate and two more guard the bridges. On either side of the bridges are reviewing stands with a capacity of 2,200 people. *Huabiao* have a long history in China. According to ancient records, one of the sage kings by the name of Yao set up a wooden pillar on which people could carve their criticisms of officials, thus showing his willingness to accept the views of the common people. This wooden pillar was the predecessor of *huabiao*. *Huabiao* later were used as boundary markers in fields, and somewhat later as tombstones and later again as road signs. Each of the white marble *huabiao* at Tiananmen weighs more than 10,000 kilogrammes. On top is a round basin for collecting dew, on which squats a stone animal called *hou*. Across the upper part of the *huabiao* is a slab of marble in the shape of a cloud. A carved dragon writhing among clouds twists around the body of the pillar. The *hou* on top of the *huabiao* in front of Tiananmen looking south are popularly known as the *wangtian hou* which gaze at heaven, its duty being to watch over the emperor's behaviour when he was outside the palace, and admonish him not to be licentious or dissolute. If the emperor was gone for too long, they would say, "O ruler of the country, do not indulge yourself outside, but return to administer the state. Our eyes are strained awaiting your return." From this they were also given the name "wangjungui", meaning "awaiting the emperor's return", and the pillars on which they squat are called "wangzhu" "awaiting pillars". The *hou* on the *huabiao* inside the gate look north towards the palace, and watched over the emperor's behaviour inside. They admonished him, "O ruler, do not always keep within the palace, enjoying the company of your empress and concubines, but go out and learn about the miseries of the common people. Our eyes are strained awaiting your emergence." They are given the name "wangjunchu", meaning "awaiting the emperor's emergence". These stories about the *huabiao* were widely known, and voiced popular sentiments in regard to the rulers. At the base of each *huabiao* are four stone lions in pairs around the *huabiao*, the males on the left playing with a stone ball with their right front paws, and the females on the right playing with a lion cub with their left front paws.

Today, the splendour of Tiananmen attracts thousands of visitors from all parts of China and abroad, but in the past, as part of the forbidden ground around the Imperial Palace, it was only for the use of the imperial court. Commoners were not even permitted to approach it, let alone pass through its passageways. The corrupt and incompetent rulers of the Qing dynasty, unable to protect China, were even unable to protect Tiananmen. During the late 19th and early 20th centuries, it was devastated by imperialist invaders. In 1900, the allied forces of the eight foreign powers shelled Tiananmen and destroyed the glazed *wenshou* on the ridges of the gate-tower. Three shell fragments with English lettering were removed from a west beam when the gate-tower was repaired in 1952.

The late Chairman Mao Zedong proclaimed the founding of the People's Republic of China from the rostrum of Tiananmen on October 1, 1949. From that moment Tiananmen achieved a new glory and came to symbolize both Beijing and China. The national emblem of the People's Republic of China has Tiananmen as its central motif, and the emblem, floodlit at night, is now suspended from the upper roof. Visitors come to admire the gate-tower, bridges, stone lions and *huabiao*, and have their photographs taken as a souvenir of their visit.

Tiananmen Square

Tiananmen Square is directly south of Tiananmen, and covers an area of 50 hectares in the heart of Beijing. It measures 500 metres from east to west and 880 metres from north to south. Because of its vastness and central location the square has become the site of grand assemblies on occasions such as International Labour Day on May 1 and China's National Day on October 1. In the centre of the square waves a bright red flag with five yellow stars, the national flag of the People's Republic of China, which was first raised by the late Chairman Mao Zedong on October 1, 1949.

Around the square are several famous buildings: Tiananmen to the north, Qianmen (Front Gate) to the south, the Great Hall of the People to the west and the Museum of the Chinese Revolution and the Museum of Chinese History to the east. The Chairman Mao Zedong Memorial Hall and the Monument to the People's Heroes stand in the southern part of the square. The Great Hall of the People, the museums and the Chairman Mao Zedong Memorial Hall are all in somewhat similar style, with flat roofs, glazed tile eaves and granite columns.

The Great Hall of the People

The Great Hall of the People is the centre of the country's political activity where the National People's Congress convenes and many other important meetings are held.   Chinese and foreign guests are entertained at banquets, receptions and memorial meetings.

Inside is a grand assembly hall, which can hold more than 10,000 people at one time.   It is 76 metres wide and 60 metres long, and has a volume of over 80,000 cubic metres.   Nearly 500 light apertures set into the vaulted ceiling give the effect of a sky full of stars. Thirty meeting rooms, one for each province, municipality and autonomous region in China, are furnished in local styles with local handicrafts.   The banquet hall, in the north wing, can seat 5,000 and has a floor space of 7,000 square metres.   The corridor pillars are covered with gold foil and there are painted coffered ceilings in the main hall and along the corridors.   The south wing contains the offices and reception rooms of the Standing Committee of the National People's Congress; it is built in the shape of a square and has several courtyards and lawns.

The Great Hall of the People in its entirety occupies 171,800 square metres and has a volume of 1,590,000 cubic metres.   It therefore is larger than the effective construction area of the whole Imperial Palace of the Ming and Qing dynasties.   Construction of the Imperial Palace took altogether 36 years, while the Great Hall of the People was erected in only ten months in 1959.

The Monument to the People's Heroes

The Monument to the People's Heroes dominates

the centre of Tiananmen Square. It symbolizes the respect of the Chinese people for their revolutionary martyrs and represents the heroic struggle of the Chinese people against internal and external enemies. The monument was erected in accordance with a resolution by the First Plenary Session of the Chinese People's Political Consultative Conference on September 30, 1949. Construction began on August 1, 1952 and was completed in April 1958. The monument was unveiled on May Day that year.

The granite obelisk, which stands on a double terrace with marble balustrades, weighs 60 tons and is 14.7 metres high. On the front side, facing Tiananmen, is an inscription in gold by the late Chairman Mao Zedong: "Eternal glory to the people's heroes." The inscription on the south side, drafted by Chairman Mao Zedong and in the handwriting of the late Premier Zhou Enlai,[1] reads:

> Eternal glory to the people's heroes who laid down their lives in the people's War of Liberation and the people's revolution in the past three years. Eternal glory to the people's heroes who laid down their lives in the people's War of Liberation and the people's revolution in the past thirty years. Eternal glory to the people's heroes who from 1840 laid down their lives in the many struggles against internal and external enemies, for national independence and the freedom and well-being of the people.

The east and west sides of the obelisk are carved with red stars, pines and cypresses, and flags, symbolizing the eternal revolutionary spirit of the martyrs. On the top is a stone roof in traditional *wudian* (thatched

[1]周恩来。

hall) style, with carved decorations of clouds above and
curtains below. *Wudian* style was formerly reserved
for the most important imperial palaces, such as the
Taihedian in the Forbidden City.

From ground to top, the monument rises 37.4 metres,
4.24 metres higher than Tiananmen; it is the biggest
monument in the country. The terrace covers an area of
more than 3,000 square metres, and the lower terrace is in
the shape of a crabapple flower. At the top of two
flights of granite stairs is a double *sumeru* plinth on
which stands the obelisk. The upper plinth is decorated
on all four sides with carvings of eight large wreathes
of peonies, lotus and chrysanthemums, symbolizing nobility, purity and perseverance. Eight white marble reliefs placed around the lower plinth depict scenes from
Chinese history since 1840: Starting from the east, these
are (1) "burning the opium" (the beginning of the Opium
War in 1840), (2) the Jintian Uprising in Guangxi (1851),
(3) the Wuchang Uprising in Hubei (the beginning of the
1911 Democratic Revolution led by Dr Sun Yat-sen), (4)
the May 4th Movement (1919), (5) the May 30th Movement (1925), (6) the Nanchang Uprising in Jiangxi (1927),
(7) guerrilla war against the Japanese invaders (1937-
45), and (8) the victorious crossing of the Changjiang
(Yangtze River) by the People's Liberation Army (1949).
The last relief, which faces north, is flanked by two
smaller reliefs: "supporting the front" and "welcoming
the People's Liberation Army". Each relief is two metres high, and altogether 170 figures are depicted. It
took China's leading sculptors and stonemasons more
than five years to complete the carving.

The Chairman Mao Zedong Memorial Hall

The Chairman Mao Zedong Memorial Hall stands between Tiananmen and Qianmen, facing north. It contains the embalmed body of the late Chairman of the Chinese Communist Party. The foundation stone was laid on November 24, 1976, and construction was finished in August 1977. It was first opened on September 9 the same year, the first anniversary of his death. Above the main entrance is a white marble tablet with the words "Chairman Mao Zedong Memorial Hall" inscribed in gold. The square hall stands on a double platform with marble balustrades. Forty-four octagonal granite columns support the double roof, with eaves of gold glazed tiles.

Four groups of sculpture stand to the side, two in front of the south entrance and two in front of the north and main entrance. The sculptures in front of the south gate include 62 figures of workers, peasants, cadres, soldiers, scientists, technicians and children. The sculpture group to the east of the north entrance represents the period of the New Democratic Revolution (1919-1949), and the group to the west represents the heroic achievements of the Chinese people in the period of socialist revolution and construction since 1949.

Around the hall is a landscaped garden planted with evergreen pines and cypresses. Flowering trees and shrubs from all parts of China fill the air with fragrance, among them pomegranates from Shaanxi, tangerines from Mao Zedong's birthplace, Shaoshan, Hunan, azaleas from Sichuan, camellias from Yunnan and thirteen pines from Yan'an in northwest China which remind people of the 13 momentous years the late Chairman spent there after the Long March of 1934-35.

Inside the Memorial Hall are three main sections. In the front is the north lobby, for the commemoration of the late Chairman, with a white marble statue, three metres high, of Chairman Mao seated in an armchair in the centre of the lobby. Behind the statue, a wool needle-point tapestry, 24 metres long, covers the back wall, depicting the vast landscape of China.

Passing through the carved side-doors of *nanmu* (a fine hardwood), one enters the central hall where the body of the late Chairman lies in state. Draped with the flag of the Chinese Communist Party, the body lies in a crystal coffin on a black marble base surrounded by banks of flowers. The body is less than two metres from the aisles so that it can clearly be seen by viewers. On the white marble south wall is an inscription in gold reading: "Eternal glory to the great leader and teacher Chairman Mao Zedong". Beyond is the south lobby, where the late Chairman's famous poem "Reply to Comrade Guo Moruo" is inscribed in gold inlay in his own handwriting on the white marble north wall. Both the poem and the powerful calligraphy are very stirring.

Outside the southern entrance, running from east to west, are thirty bright red flags, representing all the provinces (including Taiwan), municipalities and autonomous regions in China.

The Museum of the Chinese Revolution and Museum of Chinese History

Along the eastern side of Tiananmen Square is a cream building with green and yellow eaves, standing 33 metres high; the north wing houses the Museum of the Chinese Revolution and the south wing houses the Museum of Chinese History.

The Museum of the Chinese Revolution contains a two-storeyed exhibition hall with 4,000 square metres of floor space on each storey; two other halls are for special exhibitions. It is a state museum for revolutionary documents and materials on Party history dating from the May 4th Movement of 1919 and the founding of the Communist Party of China in 1921. The permanent exhibition is devoted to the history of the Communist Party of China up to 1949. At the present it concentrates on the period of the New Democratic Revolution; in the future, material on the period of socialist revolution and construction will be mounted here as well.

The exhibits on Party history in the New Democratic Revolution are divided into five sections: the founding of the Communist Party of China in 1921; the First Revolutionary Civil War (1924-27); the Second Revolutionary Civil War (1927-37); the War of Resistance Against Japan (1937-45); and the Third Revolutionary Civil War (1945-49). More than 3,300 exhibits illustrate the history of the Party up to Liberation.

Temporary exhibitions held at the museum have included the anniversary of Lenin's 90th birthday (mounted in 1960); the 20th anniversary of the victory of the War of Resistance Against Japan (1965); the centenary of the birth of Dr Sun Yat-sen (1966); the 40th anniversary of the victory of the Long March (1975); and the life of Zhou Enlai (1977).

The Museum of Chinese History has a permanent exhibition of 9,000 historic relics and documents showing the course of Chinese history. It is divided into four sections according to different stages in the development of Chinese society: primitive society (from about 600,000 years ago to the 21st century B.C.); slave society

View of Beijing with the Jianguomen flyover in the foreground.

Aerial view of the Palace Museum (Forbidden City).

Tiananmen at dawn.

The Great Wall.

The Qiniandian (Hall of Prayers for Good Harvest) at Tiantan (Altar of Heaven) where the Ming and Qing emperors worshipped heaven.

Souvenir Photographs at Tiananmen.

The newly-built Capital Airport.

Departure Hall at the Capital Airport.

A terminal at the Capital Airport.

(the 21st century B.C.-476 B.C.); feudal society (475 B.C.-1840 A.D.); and the semi-colonial, semi-feudal society of the Period of the Old Democratic Revolution (1840-1919). Exhibits in the first section include pre-historic fossils and other relics of Yuanmou Man from Yunnan, Lantian Man from Shaanxi, and Peking Man from Zhoukoudian. Other sections show fine bronzeware, jade and bone implements, drinking vessels and silk fabrics from the slave society; iron work and farm tools from early feudal society; and pottery, porcelain and many other objects from the Tang dynasty and after. The four great inventions of ancient China are shown: gunpowder, printing, the compass and paper-making, along with other achievements in ideology, culture, science and technology. Famous Chinese statesmen, philosophers, scientists, writers and artists are depicted, and the history of friendly contacts between the Chinese and people of other countries is given. There is also a rich collection of historical documents, objects and paintings which depict peasant uprisings in feudal times and the Chinese people's struggles against invasion in modern times.

3

The Palace Museum

Beijing became a capital of northern China during the Liao dynasty and a capital of a unified China during the Yuan, and for most of the Ming and all of the Qing it remained the imperial capital. The feudal emperors undertook large-scale construction projects, leaving behind a magnificent collection of palaces. The largest was the group of palaces in the heart of Beijing known as the Purple Forbidden City (purple was the symbolic colour of the North Star, the centre of the cosmos), and until after the 1911 Revolution the public was strictly denied entry. The Forbidden City is now the Palace Museum, generally referred to in Chinese as the Gugong (Ancient Palace). Construction of the palace buildings began in the fourth year of the Yongle reign (1406) of the Ming dynasty and was completed fourteen years later. Twenty-four emperors lived here over a span of more than 491 years, from its first resident Zhudi (the Yongle emperor) to Puyi, last emperor of the Qing dynasty.

The Forbidden City served the emperor as both living quarters and headquarters for the administration of the empire. The grand buildings were not only splendid in appearance but were well protected by multiple lines of defence. In Ming and Qing times, Beijing

THE PALACE MUSEUM

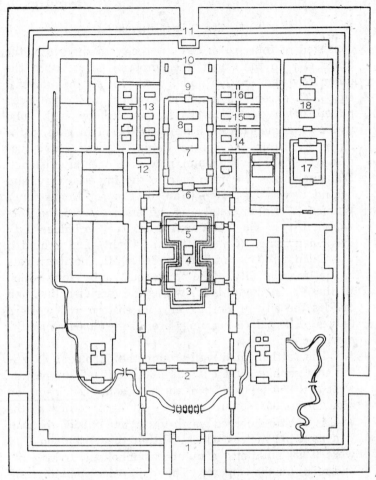

1 Wumen
2 Taihemen
3 Taihedian
4 Zhonghedian
5 Baohedian
6 Qianqingmen
7 Qianqinggong
8 Kunninggong
9 Imperial Garden
10 Qin'andian
11 Shenwumen
12 Yangxindian
13 Six Western Palaces
   for Imperial Concubines
14 Bronze Exhibition
15 Pottery and Porcelain
   Exhibition
16 Ming and Qing Handi-
   crafts Exhibition
17 Painting Exhibition
18 Gold and Jade Exhibition

consisted of four parts: the outer city to the south, the inner city to the north, the Imperial City within the inner city and the Forbidden City within the imperial city. All except the outer city, whose walls had been pulled down earlier, were surrounded by high solid walls. Qianmen (Front Gate) was the main gate to the inner city from the south. Behind it was Zhonghuamen (Central Flowery Gate), now no longer in existence. Tiananmen was the main gate to the Imperial City, and behind it was Duanmen (Gate of Correct Demeanour). Wumen (Meridian Gate) was the main gate to the Forbidden City. The main exit from the Forbidden City was Shenwumen (Gate of Divine Might), and behind it was Di'anmen (Gate of Earthly Peace), the northern gate to the Imperial City. The north-south axis, along which all these gates stand, is known as the meridian line, and divides the city of Beijing into its eastern and western halves. The palace buildings are also grouped along the meridian line.

The battlemented wall around the Forbidden City is ten metres high and extends 760 metres from east to west and 960 metres from north to south, enclosing an area of 720,000 square metres. At each corner of the wall is a three-storeyed watch-tower, and outside the wall is a moat 52 metres wide. Within the Forbidden City were 9,999 buildings, a number symbolizing a long life and reign for the emperor. The main palace buildings are on the meridian line facing south, and the less important buildings are ranged to the east and west. The front part of the Forbidden City was known as the "outer court": here the emperor received high officials and conducted the administration of the empire; behind it is the "inner court", where the emperor lived with his consorts; and to the rear is the imperial garden, where the imperial family could pass their leisure time.

Wumen, also known as Wufenglou (Five Phoenix Tower), is the main and south gate to the palace. Its red platform is ten metres high and is flanked by massive wings to the east and west. The main gate-tower is nine bays wide and has a double roof in *wudian* style with four fully hipped sides covered with yellow glazed tiles. On each wing are two square pavilions connected by covered galleries and roofed with yellow glazed tiles. These are the "five phoenixes". With its three great platforms and five massive towers, Wumen is the most forbidding portal in the palace.

During the Qing dynasty, the civil and military officials in the capital would wait inside Wumen every morning for the emperor to appear in court. The emperor's arrival would be announced by the drums and bells in the pavilions on other side of the tower gate. When the emperor left the palace to perform sacrificial rites at Tiantan or Ditan (altars of heaven and earth), the bells were rung, and when he went to the Taimiao to offer sacrifices to his ancestors, the drums were beaten. When a general returned from battle, his captives would be "offered" in a ceremony here. During the Ming dynasty, it was also the site of floggings of officials who had incurred the emperor's disfavour.

Beyond Wumen are the five Inner Golden Water Bridges with white marble balustrades, which lead to Taihemen (Gate of Supreme Harmony). Inside this gate are the three main halls of the outer court. The three halls stand on a three-tiered, balustraded terrace of white marble, known as the "dragon pavement". Side buildings to the east and west form a square courtyard.

In each corner of the courtyard is a square tower, used as a watchtower by the imperial guards.

The first and main hall is the Taihedian (Hall of Supreme Harmony), from where the emperor exercised his rule over the state; it is the most striking building in the entire palace. Here the emperor ascended the throne, received high officials and celebrated important festivals. It is not only a splendid example of ancient Chinese architecture and design, but also one of the finest wooden buildings left to us from ancient times. During the Ming and Qing dynasties, it was the tallest building in Beijing, standing 35.05 metres high — 37.44 metres if the rooftop decoration is counted. The law of the time forbade officials and commoners to have homes higher than the palace. The hall is 63.96 metres wide and 37.20 metres deep, and contains 72 pillars standing in six rows (including the walls). The traditional way of calculating the interior space of a building is to count the square enclosed by four pillars as one room, so this hall can be said to have 55 "rooms". The six gold-lacquered pillars standing in the middle are 14.4 metres tall and 1.06 metres in diameter, and are carved with coiled dragons. Enclosed within the pillars is the throne, which stands on a *sumeru* dias two metres high. The dias is also decorated with gilded coiled dragons. The "dragon table" and imperial throne are gilded and carved in a cloud and dragon pattern. Above the throne is a gilded coffered ceiling with a traditional design of dragons toying with pearls. Behind the throne is a intricately carved screen. Around the throne stand two bronze cranes, an elephant-shaped incense burner and tripods in the shape of mythical beasts. In front of the dias are four cloisonne incense burners.

In feudal China, not only people but roofs were divided into ranks. Because the Taihedian was the emperor's throne hall, the seat of the exercise of his power, its roof had to be of the highest rank, in the *wudian* (thatched hall) style with four fully-hipped double roofs with curved overhanging eaves. The roof decorations are also of the highest rank: like the Tiananmen gate-tower, it has *zhengwen* and *wenshou* on the central and side ridges, but the *zhengwen* are much bigger, each weighing 4,250 kilogrammes, and there are two more *wenshou* on each of the side ridges.

A three-tiered staircase, eight metres high, leads up to the hall. It is called the *danchi* (cinnabar staircase). The long stone ramp carved with dragons sporting in clouds in bas-relief in the centre of the staircase was reserved for the emperor's use only; imperial relatives and officials had to climb the forty-four steps to either side. Along the base of the balustrade are 1,142 marble waterspouts in the shape of dragons' heads, which spout gushes of water during heavy rain. Arranged around the terrace in front of the hall are a sundial and a grain-measure, indicating the emperor's concern for agriculture, four bronze incense burners in the shapes of tortoises and cranes, symbols of longevity, six bronze tripod (*ding*) incense burners and four large bronze cauldrons for storing water in case of fire (a frequent hazard in the mainly wooden structures of the palace) and also suggesting the perfection of the emperor's reign.

In front of the Taihedian is a vast empty courtyard with an area of more than 30,000 square metres. The grand scale of the courtyard was necessary to accommodate the large numbers of civil and military officials who would assemble here for important ceremonies. Arrayed according to rank, they would kneel down as guards of honour stood by. The emperor, seated on his throne, was wreathed in fragrant clouds of incense rising from the bronze crane and tortoise incense burners and tripods inside and outside the hall, creating an aura of mystery around him. The imposing surroundings and atmosphere were designed to strike awe into the subjects of the "Son of Heaven".

Behind the Taihedian is the Zhonghedian (Hall of Central Harmony), a small square building with a single pyramidic roof. It contains a throne, tripods and incense burners. This hall served as a resting place for the emperor on his way to the Taihedian. He received members of the cabinet and officials in the Ministry of Rites, and rehearsals for ceremonies were also held here.

The last of the three great outer halls is the Baohedian (Hall of Preserved Harmony), second to only the Taihedian in grandeur and spaciousness. Its roof is in the *xieshan* style used for the Tiananmen gate-tower, and it contains another throne with gilded carving. Here the emperor gave banquets to princes of vassal states on the lunar New Year's Eve. During the Qing dynasty, the emperor also supervised here the final stage of examinations to select officials from among scholars from all over the country. A similar three-tiered staircase with a central imperial ramp leads down behind the Baohedian to the courtyard below. The ramp consists of a 16 metre-long white marble slap weighing more than 200 tons, carved with a dragon flying amid clouds.

On either side of the Taihemen, outside the courtyard south of the Taihedian, stands a group of important buildings. To the east is the Wenhuadian (Hall of Literary Glory), which served as a study for the crown

prince during the Ming dynasty. The Ming and Qing
emperors also attended lectures here in spring and
autumn. Behind it is the Wenyuange (Pavilion of the
Source of Literature), the Qing imperial library where
the famous collection *Siku Quanshu*[1] (Complete Library
of the Four Treasures of Knowledge) was formerly
housed. Further east are the Qing Archives. The
principal building to the west is the Wuyingdian (Hall
of Martial Valour) where the empress received her
female subjects during the Ming dynasty. At the end
of the Ming dynasty, Li Zicheng held his coronation
here after he led his peasant army into Beijing. During
the Qing dynasty, it was the office where scholars compiled the *Siku Quanshu,* the *Peiwen Yunfu,*[2] a diction-
ary compiled according to Chinese rhymes, and the *Gu-
jintushu Jicheng,*[3] an anthology of famous writings. It
was also the site of the imperial printing presses. Another important building here is the Nanxundian (South
Fragrance Hall), one of the few remaining buildings
from the Ming; portraits of emperors of various dynasties are stored here.

The inner palace, or residential quarters of the imperial family, is entered through Qianqingmen (Gate of
Celestial Purity). In front of this gate stand two gilded
bronze lions and on each side is a gilded bronze cauldron.
During the Qing dynasty, a throne was placed at the
gate for the emperor to hear reports from high officials
and issue his decisions: this illustrates the personal style
of the Qing emperors in administration, and was called
"governing the state under an imperial gate". The practice was abandoned in the last days of the Qing. When
the allied forces of the eight powers invaded Beijing

[1]《四库全书》；[2]《佩文韵府》；[3]《古今图书集成》。

and forced their way into the imperial palace in 1900, they scraped much of the gold off the bronze cauldrons; scratches left by their bayonets are still visible.

The living quarters of the imperial family, concubines, maids and eunuchs in the inner court can be roughly divided into three parts: three main buildings in the centre, six halls to the east and six halls to the west; they are usually known as "the three palaces and the six courtyards". The three rear palaces, like the three great halls of the outer court, stand on a large stone terrace, but the terrace and the halls, as well as the buildings to the each side, are on a much smaller scale. The first of the three palaces is the Qianqinggong (Palace of Celestial Purity). It is 9 bays long and 5 bays deep, and in the centre is a throne. This was the emperor's bedroom, but was also used for day-to-day administration and for reading memorials. On festival days, the emperor gave large banquets here. The empress' bedchamber was the third of the main palaces, at the rear of the terrace, and was called the Kunninggong (Palace of Terrestrial Tranquillity). During the Qing, it was used as the emperor's bridal chamber. Outside the east wall is a sedan chair covered with red and yellow satin, in which the empress was carried around the palace grounds. Between the two halls is the smaller Jiaotaidian (Hall of Celestial and Terrestrial Union), for lesser-scale ceremonies such as empress' birthday. In spring, the empress would raise silkworms here to show her industry and capability, to set an example for her women subjects. During the Qing dynasty, it was used to store the official seals of the emperor and empress; today, there are still twenty-five imperial seals on ex-

hibit here, together with traditional Chinese clepsydra
(water-clocks) and a Western clock.

The Qianqinggong represents the heavens, the
Kunninggong represents earth and the Jiaotaidian represents their union. The Rijingmen and Yuehuamen, two
gates in front of the Qianqinggong, represent the sun
and the moon. All these symbolized that the emperor's
reign was as eternal and glorious as the universe.

The twelve courtyards around the three central
palaces were inhabited by concubines, dowagers and
maids. They also held Buddhist shrines and collections
of various treasures. The buildings are arranged in two
rows on either side of a south-north axis. At the southern end of the eastern courtyards are the Fengxian-
dian (Hall for Ancestral Worship), an imperial ancestral
temple, and the Zhaigong (Palace of Abstinence), where
the emperor practised abstinence from meat the day before going to offer sacrifices at the Altar of Heaven or
the Altar of Earth. These two halls and five palaces
which were inhabited by concubines, the Jingrengong
(Palace of Great Benevolence), Chengqiangong (Palace
of Celestial Favour), Yonghegong (Palace of Eternal
Harmony), Jingyanggong (Palace of Great Brilliance) and
Zhongcuigong (Palace of Purity), have now become exhibition halls for traditional Chinese arts. Behind the
six palaces were storehouses for tea and brocade, and to
the north were kitchens. In a separate enclosure further
east are two palace halls where Qianlong lived after
his abdication and later inhabited by Cixi, the Empress
Dowager; these are the Huangjidian (Hall of Imperial Su-
premacy), a smaller replica of the Qianqinggong, and the
Ningshougong (Palace of Tranquil Longevity), a smaller
replica of the Kunninggong. These two halls now hold

the famous collections of Chinese paintings whose treasures are shown in annual rotation. North of these halls
are three more, the private apartments of Qianlong and
Cixi: the Yangxingdian (Hall for Cultivating Character),
presumably named after Qianlong's western apartment,
the Yangxindian (Hall of Mental Cultivation); the Leshoutang (Hall of Joyful Longevity), a library; and the
Yihexuan (Pavilion of Sustained Harmony). The Empress Dowager used to receive foreign women in the
Yangxingdian, and used the Leshoutang as a bedchamber. These three halls are now used for an exhibition
of jewellery.

The six courtyards to the west, formally inhabited
by concubines, now hold an exhibition presenting a picture of Qing palace life. The Tiyuandian (Hall of Manifest Origin) and the Changchundian (Palace of Eternal
Spring), where the Empress Dowager once lived as a con-
cubine, have been left in their original condition. To the
south and southeast of these two are the Taijidian (Hall
of the Supreme Pole) and the Yongshougong (Palace of
Eternal Longevity), also inhabited by concubines. To the
north are four more apartments for concubines, the Xian-
fugong (Palace of Universal Happiness), the Yikungong
(Palace of the Queen Consort), the Tihedian (Hall of
Manifest Harmony) and the Chuxiugong (Palace for
Gathering Elegance), where the last emperor's wife
lived. These are now exhibition halls for Qing arts and
handicrafts.

The Yangxindian (Hall of Mental Cultivation), southwest of the three rear palaces, deserves special mention.
The Yongzheng emperor moved into this building in
1723, abandoning the official imperial residence, the
Qianqinggong (Palace of Celestial Purity). For nearly

two hundred years until the fall of the dynasty in 1911, all subsequent Qing emperors lived and attended to affairs of state in this hall. In front of the Yangxindian is a pair of gilded bronze lions. On the staircase leading up to the door is a small *danchi* slab carved with dragons and clouds, indicating an imperial residence. Inside are a throne and table, and above is an octagonal coffered ceiling in a dragon design. Incense burners and tripods stand to the each side of the table. The Dongnuange (Eastern Warmth Chamber) in the Yangxindian is where the two empresses dowagers, Cixi and Cian,[1] attended to affairs of state from behind a screen, while in front sat the boy emperors, Tongzhi and Guangxu. Later, Guangxu's widow, the Empress Dowager Longyu,[2] similarly held court while the last Qing emperor, Puyi, sat in front. In the Xinuange (Western Warmth Chamber), the emperor received his defence minister and other trusted officials. To the west of this chamber is the Sanxitang (Room of Three Rarities), where manuscripts by famous Chinese calligraphers collected by the Qianlong emperor are stored.

North of the three rear palaces and six courtyards is the Yuhuayuan (Imperial Garden). It is small in area but exquisitely laid out with towers, pavilions, an artificial hill, rocks, springs, ancient cypresses, flowers and shrubs.

Behind the garden is the Shenwumen (Gate of Divine Might), originally called the Xuanwumen (Gate of Occult Might), the rear gate of the Forbidden City. The gate-tower formerly contained drums and bells. Every day at dusk, the bells would toll 108 times. After that

[1]慈安；[2]隆裕。

the drums would beat to tell the hour at each watch of the night until again the bell sounded 108 times at sunrise.

In the 491 years from 1420 to 1911, the imperial palace was the political centre of China under the Ming and Qing emperors. After the 1911 Revolution, Emperor Puyi resigned and the government of the republic took possession of the three main halls of the outer palace, plus the Wenhuadian and Wuyingdian, and set up an Antiquities Exhibition Hall inside the palace in 1914. Puyi and his courtiers continued to live in the inner palace. After Puyi was finally driven out in 1925, the Palace Museum was formally set up in October the same year. But owing to bad management, the palace was not well cared for, and many buildings fell into ruin and the courtyards became overgrown with weeds. After the liberation of Beijing in 1949, the people's government placed the palace under its protection and allocated funds for its renovation. With its magnificent halls and courtyards and its imperial collections of arts and antiques, the whole palace is now a museum of world importance for Chinese history, culture and art. It was declared a major national treasure under state protection in 1961.

4

The Hill Station at Chengde[1]

Historical Background

Chengde (Jehol),[2] a city 250 kilometres northeast of Beijing, is situated amid some of the most beautiful scenery in north China. The second emperor of the Qing dynasty, Kangxi, set up an imperial summer resort here in 1703, and construction of the palaces, gardens and temples was completed under his grandson, the Qianlong emperor. The Bishushanzhuang (Hill Station to Escape the Heat), as Kangxi named his resort, occupies 5.6 million square metres and has the largest and best preserved imperial palace outside Beijing. It is popularly known as the Rehe Xinggong or Chengde Ligong (Jehol or Chengde Summer Palace).

Kangxi and Qianlong were frequent visitors to the Mulan (*Manchu*: hunting deer by imitating the deer's cry) hunting grounds, built by Kangxi for the purpose of military training, some 400 kilometres northeast of Beijing. Between Beijing and Mulan were 19 imperial resorts, of which the Chengde Hill Station was the largest and the best. Apart from recreation, the Qing emperors also used the Chengde Hill Station as an administrative centre, especially in regard to relations with the regions to the north and northwest, and as a military

[1]承德；[2]热河。

headquarters for defending the border in the north. As a result of the frequent and extended imperial visits, Chengde developed from a small village into a city of nearly 100,000.

Chengde is in the Luan River[1] valley in the northeast of Hebei. A tributary of the Luan, the Wulie River,[2] formerly the Rehe (Jehol) River, flows to the east of the town and the Hill Station. The small valley is surrounded by picturesquely shaped mountains belonging to the Yanshan range to the west and the Xin'an range to the north, and lies about 380 metres above sea level. Its protected situation moderates the harsh continental climate and strong winds of north China, giving it an average temperature of 24°C in July and −9°C in January.

Chengde was originally known as Rehe (Jehol) after the Rehe River: the name means "warm river", and in fact the river does not freeze over in winter. Excavations show that the area was inhabited in the later stages of primitive society. From Qin and Han times it was occupied by the Xiongnu,[3] Qidan and other northern tribes. After Kangxi established the Hill Station a township gradually grew up to provide its services. It became the administrative centre of eastern Mongolia in 1724 in the Yongzheng reign and the name Chengde was first used in 1733. After 1742, in the Qianlong reign, the population of Chengde increased rapidly. At the beginning of the Qing dynasty, prohibitions on the use of land for agriculture and industry restricted the area's development, but the lifting of some of these restrictions by Qianlong brought the population up to 460,000 by 1782. The first school was set up in 1746.

[1]滦河；[2]武烈河；[3]匈奴。

CHENGDE HILL STATION AND THE EIGHT OUTER TEMPLES

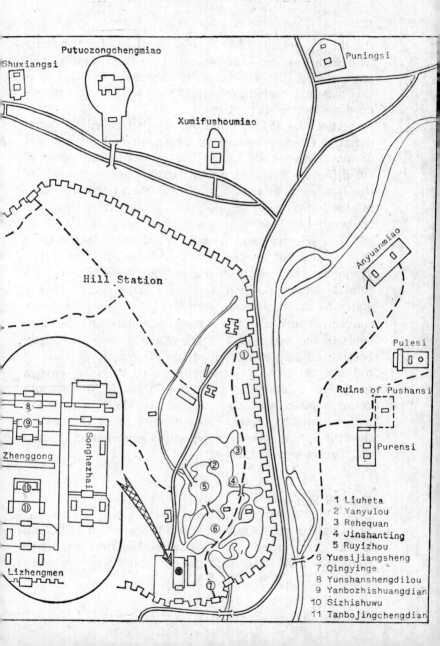

Shuxiangsi

Putuozongchengmiao

Puningsi

Xumifushoumiao

Anyuanmiao

Hill Station

Pulesi

Ruins of Pushansi

Purensi

Zhenggong

Songhezhai

Lizhengmen

1 Liuheta
2 Yanyulou
3 Rehequan
4 **Jinshanting**
5 Ruyizhou
6 Yuesijiangsheng
7 Qingyinge
8 Yunshanshengdilou
9 Yanbozhishuangdian
10 Sizhishuwu
11 Tanbojingchengdian

By the second half of the nineteenth century, mining was permitted and land was diverted from hunting and pastoral use to agriculture; by this time, the Hill Station was in a period of decline, but the town had developed an independent economy.

After the 1911 Revolution which toppled the Qing dynasty, Chengde entered a long period of neglect and decay. Between 1911 and 1932, it was in the hands of six different warlords, and in 1933 it was occupied by the Japanese. Liberated in 1945, it then became a Kuomintang stronghold in the War of Liberation, and was reliberated in 1948.

The selection and growth of this area in the Qing dynasty was not accidental. As early as 1677, the Kangxi emperor had established a military base here to consolidate Qing rule over the tribal lands and tributary states to the north and northwest. It also provided a convenient link with the Manchu homelands of the Qing court in the northeast. In the Qianlong reign, Chengde became an important centre for diplomatic as well as military activity, where the emperor received envoys from Tibet, Mongolia and even England. To promote better relations with the Tibetans and Mongolians, Qianlong established several Lama temples north and east of the Hill Station, which incorporated elements of Tibetan and Turkic architectural styles.

The Hill Station

Construction began on the Hill Station in 1703, and it was given its present name when the first stage was completed in 1708. During the remaining fourteen years of his life, Kangxi came here forty-eight times, and suggestions that he was getting too old for hunting met his vigorous opposition. His successor, the Yongzheng emperor, never came here himself, though he encouraged his son, the future Qianlong emperor, to keep up the family traditions in hunting and the martial arts. In the sixth year of his reign (1741), Qianlong greatly enlarged the Hill Station and at the same time expanded the political importance of the resort. It was at this time that the new temples were built; apart from the Confucian temple in Chengde itself (the remains of which can still be seen), and the Taoist and Buddhist temples within the Hill Station for the private use of the court, Qianlong constructed seven Lama temples here and promoted Lamaism to the status of a national religion. Within the Hill Station, he initiated a building programme that was not completed until 1790: to the thirty-six sights enumerated by Kangxi, he added another thirty-six. Between 1741 and 1751 he came here once every two years, and from 1751 to his death in 1795, he spent half of each year here, conducting court business, celebrating his birthday, meeting foreign envoys and tribal chiefs and preparing for hunting at Mulan.

After Qianlong, the Hill Station gradually fell out of favour with the Qing court. The Jiaqing emperor died here in 1820, and his successor Daoguang thought little of the area's attractions. On the Anglo-French occupation of Beijing in 1860, the Xianfeng emperor fled here and died the following year. After this the Hill Station was abandoned, and over the next hundred years the palaces and grounds were reduced almost to ruins. In 1961, the Hill Station and four of the outlying temples were designated national treasures under state protection, and reconstruction and renovation have restored much of their former splendour.

The Hill Station is situated to the northeast of Chengde city, on the west bank of the Wulie River. It is now a large park, surrounded by a battlemented wall, open to the public in the daytime and at evening. It occupies an area of 560 hectares, roughly the same size as the Yuanmingyuan and much bigger than the Yiheyuan in the western suburbs of Beijing. Ancient pines and cypresses dominate the grounds, and willows line the lakes and embankments; the charm of south China landscapes is combined with the ruggedness of the north.

The Hill Station can be divided into four main areas: the palaces, the lake, the plains and the hills. The palaces and the lake are the major attractions; the plains and the hills have lost most of their original charm.

The Palaces

The palaces are to the south and southeast of the compound, near the main entrance and the town. Modelled after the Imperial City, the buildings are formal and grand, but still have an air of rural simplicity. They are arranged in four groups: the Zhenggong (Main Palace), the Songhezhai (Pine and Crane Chambers), the Wanhesongfeng (The Wind from the Valleys) and the Donggong (East Palace).

The Zhenggong consists of a series of successive courtyards leading from south to north. Entry is through the Lizhengmen (Gate of Splendour and Propriety), which is also the main entrance to the Hill Station. Built in 1754, it bears a signboard inscribed in Manchu, Mongolian, Chinese, Uyghur and Tibetan. Inside the Lizhengmen is another gate, the Wumen (Meridian Gate), followed by the Zhenggongmen (Main Palace Gate) on which is a tablet inscribed "Hill Station to Escape the Heat" in Kangxi's handwriting.

The front courtyards and halls of the Main Palace were for conducting official business, and the rear section was for the emperors' private use; the whole area is enclosed by a wall, and the arrangement of the buildings is relatively formal and symmetrical. It has now been converted into a museum: some of its halls have been maintained in their original condition, while others house collections of historical materials, hunting equipment, porcelain and so on.

The first and most imposing hall in the front section is the Tanbojingchengdian (Hall of Tranquillity and Reverence). It was first constructed by Kangxi in 1710 and rebuilt by Qianlong in 1754 out of *nanmu* (a fine hardwood). The wood is left unpainted to show off its natural beauty, and the carving of the latticed doors, windows and ceiling is particularly fine. The ancient pines in the spacious paved courtyard blends with the carved, unpainted wood to create an atmosphere of rustic elegance. This hall was only used for more formal occasions, such as the emperors' birthdays and the reception of foreign envoys and tribal chiefs. Behind the Tanbojingchengdian is the Sizhishuwu (Chamber of the Four Wisdoms); built in 1710, it was used for receptions and banquets — the Sixth Panchen Erdeni,[1] one of the two political and religious leaders in Tibet (the other being the Dalai Lama), and the chief of the Torguts were received here.

The most important building in the rear section is the Yanbozhishuangdian (Hall of Refreshing Mists and

[1] 班禅额尔德尼。

Waves), the emperors' bedchamber. It was here that the Xianfeng emperor ordered his younger brother Yixin[1] (better known to the West as Prince Kung) to sign the unequal "Treaty of Peking" with France and Germany and the "Sino-Russian Treaty of Peking" with Russia in 1860; the documents bearing his vermilion approval are displayed on the *kang* (brick-bed) table. After Xianfeng's death at the Hill Station the following year, his secondary wife Cixi here plotted with Yixin the coup d'etat that elevated her to be regent to the new emperor, her son. She later removed the entire contents of this bedchamber to Beijing. Behind the Yanbozhishuangdian is the Yunshanshengdilou (Tower of the Clouds and Mountains Resort), a two-storeyed building that marks the end and highest point of the Main Palace. Entry to the second storey is through an artificial hill in the courtyard. To the east is an entrance to the adjoining Songhezhai; behind is the northern exit, the Xiuyunmen (Cave and Cloud Gate).

The Songhezhai, in a parallel enclosure to the east of the Main Palace, was the residence of Qianlong's mother and his concubines. On a smaller scale than the Main Palace, it was built in 1749. That year the pines were very green and the cranes numerous; since both pines and cranes are symbols of longevity, it was appropriate for Qianlong to name the Empress Dowager's apartments after them. It became Jiaqing's residence after 1790 and was later burnt down. This palace is not open to the public at present.

The Wanghesongfeng, situated northeast of the Main Palace, behind the Songhezhai, was the first to be built among the palaces. Built in the style of the Xiequyuan

[1]奕訢。

in the Yiheyuan, it is a free grouping of buildings connected by covered corridors. The elegant vertical design of the latticed walls and corridors give unity to the unenclosed, unsymmetrical buildings. The main hall stands on a ridge overlooking the lake. The emperors would come here to read, study documents, receive courtiers or simply enjoy the scenery. In 1722 when the Kangxi emperor would come here to examine memorials to the throne, his twelve-year-old grandson, Aisin-Gioro Hongli, was his constant companion and beneficiary of his personal instruction. After he had ascended the throne as the Qianlong emperor, Hongli named this hall Ji'entang (Hall in Memory of Benevolence) to commemorate his grandfather and wrote an inscription on it.

The East Palace lies on a lower site to the southeast of the Main Palace and has its own entrance through the outer wall; behind it is the lake. The original buildings, which included a three-storeyed theatre (built in 1754), were destroyed in a great fire in 1948, but from the remaining foundations its grand and extensive layout can be seen. One building to the rear was destroyed in 1933 during the Japanese occupation and was restored in 1979.

The Lake

The lake area, covering 55 hectares, is the chief attraction of the Hill Station apart from the palaces. It is modelled after the famous landscape gardens and scenery of the lower Changjiang (Yangtze River) valley in south-central China. Although not far from the city, it has a delightful rural air with its lush undergrowth, ancient pines and lakeside willows. Pavilions, kiosks and halls are scattered throughout the area, adding their beauty to the natural landscape and affording fine views across the lake. The lake as a whole is known as Saihu (Border Lake), and embraces seven smaller lakes formed by islands and embankments. Some of the buildings, such as the Yanyulou (Tower of Mist and Rain), have the lively grace of the southern style; others, such as the buildings on Ruyizhou (Pleasure Island), are in the severer and plainer style of the north. The chief attractions are concentrated around the middle of the area, which includes Ruyizhou, Huanbidao, Qingliandao and Jinshan.

The Ruyizhou (Pleasure Island) is the biggest island and has the most buildings. Like the Main Palace, it was used by the emperors both for private recreation and for official receptions. Among its northern-style courtyards are the Yanxunshanguan (Rural Hall for Receiving Honoured Guests), where Kangxi and Qianlong received Mongolian princes and chieftains, a theatre and the secluded Guanliansuo (Water-Lilies View).

South of the Pleasure Island is the Zhiyingzhou, on which were a group of halls called Huanbi (Round Wall) built by Kangxi but are no longer extant. On the northern tip of the island is the thatched-roofed Cailingdu (Landing for Gathering Water-Chestnuts), where the palace ladies could board boats to go out on the lake. To the east is a causeway modelled after the famous Su Dongbo Causeway on the West Lake in Hangzhou;[1] willows grow along the embankment and across the lake the mountains come into view.

Northeast of the Pleasure Island is Qingliandao (Green Water-Lily Island), whose main building is the Yanyulou (Tower of Mist and Rain). Modelled after the building of the same name at the South Lake, in Jiaxing,[2] Zhe-

[1]杭州; [2]嘉兴。

jiang, it was built in 1780-1781 as a place where one could enjoy the rain. To one side is an artificial hill; to the other is the Qingyangshuwu (Aspen Study), with a terrace in front and a pavilion behind, where Qianlong would go to read or study.

The Jinshan (Golden Hill), east of the Pleasure Island, is surrounded by the lake on three sides and separated from the mainland by a stream, and is dominated by an artificial hill. The buildings here are modelled after Jinshan in Zhenjiang,[1] Jiangsu. On the hillside is the Fahaidong (Cave of the Sea of the Law), and on top of the hill are two buildings, the Tianyuxianchangdian (Hall of Universal Joy) and the Shangdige (Supreme Emperor Pavilion), popularly known as the Jinshanting (Golden Hill Pavilion). The three-storeyed Jinshanting is the highest structure in the lake area. It was used by the emperors for performing sacrificial rites to two important Taoist deities, the Great Jade Emperor and the Great True and Militant Emperor.

To the northeast of the Jinshan is the Rehequan (Warm River Spring), one of the main water sources of the lake. The spring does not freeze in winter, and when the sun rises a mist forms above it. North of the spring is a dock for berthing the pleasure boats for excursions on the lake.

The Plain

North of the lake is the plain, originally landscaped after the north China grasslands. It consists of three main areas, of which the most famous is the Wanshu-yuan (Park of Ten Thousand Trees). Formerly this was a vast forest carpeted with grass, where deer grazed and

[1]镇江。

birds sang among the trees. Yurts were constructed for staging feasts, wrestling matches, firework displays, horse trials and concerts featuring tribal music. The English envoy Lord Macartney and the Sixth Panchen Erdeni were received here by Qianlong. This area has been deforested and is now occupied by dormitories.

To the east of the Wanshuyuan were a group of Buddhist temples, the Imperial Portrait Gallery and the gardens, where scholars compiled encyclopedic works under imperial patronage, have also been destroyed and the area put to other uses. The Shelita (Sarira Pagoda), modelled after the Baoensita (Gratitude Temple Pagoda) in Nanjing and the Liuheta (Six Harmonies Pagoda) of the Wulingsi in Hangzhou, can still be seen in the northeast quarter and appears to be in good condition, though it is inaccessible to visitors.

To the west of Wanshuyuan is the Shimadai (Horse Trials Field), where horses were tried out for the hunt before the court set out for Mulan. Mongolian chiefs and court officials also practised riding and archery here. This area is also occupied by dormitories and a small enclosure houses the remaining deer.

Northwest of the Shimadai is the Wenjinge (Literary Ford Pavilion), built in 1774 after the famous Tianyige in Ningbo,[1] Zhejiang. Designed as a book repository, it appears to have two storeys from the outside but actually has a story in between carefully screened for the protection of the books inside. One of its most famous possessions was the *Siku Quanshu* (Complete Library of the Four Treasuries of Knowledge), a huge encyclopedic collection of ancient and modern works sponsored by Qianlong and compiled between 1773 and 1781 by over

[1]宁波。

160 scholars. Four copies were made and stored in north China libraries, and in 1787 a further three copies were made and stored in southern libraries. The copy kept at the Yuanmingyuan was destroyed in 1860. In 1915, the Chengde copy was removed to the Beijing Library and the street in front of the library is still called Wenjinjie to commemorate the original home of this priceless manuscript. In 36,304 volumes, the *Siku Quanshu* is the largest collection in China and one of the largest in the world. A rockery, pond and terrace stand in front of the pavilion.

The Hills

The hill area takes up four-fifths of the whole Hill Station and extends from the northwest border down to the lakeside. In winter it protects the rest of the park from the bitter winds. From north to south are the five main gullies: Songyunxia (Pine and Cloud Gorge), Lishugu (Peartree Gully), Songlingu (Pine Forest Gully), Zhenzigu (Hazelnut Gully) and Xigu (West Gully). In the days of Kangxi and Qianlong, there were forty-four sites here with gardens, temples and pavilions. Among them was the Zhuyuansi (Temple of the Source of the Pearl) in Peartree Gully, which contained an exquisitely carved bronze pavilion called the Zongjingge (Ancestral Mirror Pavilion) cast out of 205 tons of bronze. In the spring of 1945, it was plundered by the Japanese, who left only a bronze tablet and two bronze pillar-plates which are now on display in the museum. In Hazelnut Gully were two courtyards where Kangxi's mother once lived, but these and all the other buildings in the hills have been destroyed and only the foundations are left. The pavilion on top of one hill was recently restored. In summer, the hills support a dense undergrowth, but only vestiges remain of the original forests and groves.

The Eight Outer Temples

To the north and east of the Hill Station eleven magnificent temples were built during the Kangxi and Qianlong reigns. As they were located beyond the Great Wall and came under eight different administrations, they were usually referred to as the "Eight Outer Temples". Seven are still standing today. Two of the original eleven, the Purensi and Pushansi, were built during the Kangxi reign; the former is in poor condition and the latter no longer exists. Four of the larger Qianlong temples are better preserved, and in 1961 were designated national treasures under state protection: the Puningsi, Pulesi, Putuozongchengmiao and Xumifushoumiao. Extensive renovation began on these temples in 1979. Two other Qianlong temples, the Anyuanmiao and Shuxiangsi, are in poor condition, and three others, the Luohantang, Guang'ansi and Puyousi, no longer exist.

The Eight Outer Temples include elements of Chinese, Manchu, Mongolian and Tibetan architectural styles, symbolizing the unity of China's different ethnic groups. Most have steles or tablets bearing inscriptions by the Kangxi or Qianlong emperor in Manchu, Chinese, Mongolian and Tibetan recording the background to their construction and the historical and political events of the time. Like the Hill Station, Qianlong used the Eight Outer Temples to consolidate Qing rule over tribal lands, tributary states and protectorates in the north and northwest.

The temples are situated on the hillsides around the

Hill Station and command impressive views over the valley. Most were built on a very grand scale, and consist of two sections: a front section of two or more courtyards in traditional Chinese style, with a front gate, bell and drum towers, devaraja hall and main hall; and a rear section, on a higher elevation, in Tibetan style. All are Lama temples though not all supported a resident lama community. Together they constitute the largest centre of Lamaism outside Tibet. (For further details on Buddhist and Lama temples in Beijing, see Chapter 7.)

The temples to the east of the Hill Station will be described first, followed by the temples to the north.

The Puningsi (Temple of Universal Tranquillity)

The Puningsi is the most northerly of the eastern group of temples and stands to the west of the Wulie River on a site covering 33,000 square metres. Popularly known as the Dafosi (Great Buddha Temple), it is famous for its huge Guanyin statue, and its halls and general layout are appropriately grand.

In the late seventeenth century, the Zungars,[1] a western Mongol tribe, gained control over much of Xinjiang (Chinese Turkestan) and Inner Mongolia, and also made inroads into Tibet. Kangxi destroyed much of their power in his 1697 expedition, but it was not until 1755-57 under Qianlong that they were finally crushed. To celebrate a major victory in 1755, Qianlong ordered the construction of a lamasery in Chengde that year and named it the Puningsi in the hope that the people of the Tarim Basin, north of Tianshan, would forever live

[1] 准噶尔。

in peace. Tibetan Lamaism had by that time become the main religion of the Mongols.

The temple's first section, arranged symmetrically along a north-south axis, is typical of Samgharama in Chinese temple architecture. It includes the front gate, a stele pavilion, bell and drum towers and a devaraja hall in the first courtyard, and the main hall and side halls in the second. The pavilion contains steles inscribed by Qianlong in Manchu, Mongolian, Chinese and Tibetan: the one in the centre describes the significance of the temple while the side ones record how the Zungars were suppressed. The four devarajas are very impressive, but the figure of Veda behind the screen is missing. The double-roofed Mahavira Hall is the main hall in the second courtyard; inside are three massive Buddhas representing the three ages, Kasyapa, Sakyamuni and Maitreya. Along the side walls are the eighteen arhats. On the east and west walls are well-preserved murals of arhats and on the north wall is a mural of the eight bodhisattvas. These colourful and vivid murals are considered masterpieces of Qing art.

The mushroom-shaped rear section of the temple is built on a huge platform, nine metres high in front. The layout of this section is modelled after the Samye Monastery built in 779, the earliest Buddhist monastery in Tibet. Both Chinese and Tibetan elements are incorporated in this section. The whole structure is a *mandala*, a magic circle within a square which represents Buddhist cosmology. The main building, the Dachengzhige (Hall of Mahayana, the Great Vehicle), symbolizes Sumeru, the mountain at the centre of the Buddhist world, and houses the huge Guanyin statue. It is ringed with four sets of buildings. Closest to the main hall are

P U N I N G S I

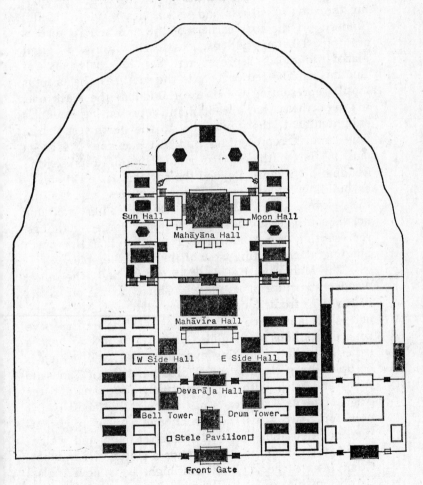

Sun Hall   Moon Hall

Mahāyāna Hall

Mahāvīra Hall

W Side Hall   E Side Hall

Devarāja Hall

Bell Tower   Drum Tower

Stele Pavilion

Front Gate

two rectangular, two-storeyed halls, the one to the east representing the moon and the one to the west representing the sun, which rise and set on either side of Mount Sumeru. At the four corners of the hall and its terrace are four Tibetan-style pagodas, each with a different glazed-tile motif, representing the "four wisdoms" of Buddhism. The red pagoda, to the southeast, has a lotus motif, representing the birth of Buddha; the black one, to the northeast, has a wand motif, representing Buddha's enlightenment; the white one, to the northwest, has a wheel motif, representing Buddhist doctrine; the green one, to the southwest, has a niche motif, representing Buddha in Nirvana. Beyond the pagodas are eight smaller buildings of different shapes and sizes, representing the "eight lesser continents". On the outer rim, due north, south, east and west, are four larger buildings, representing the "four greater continents"; the north building affords a fine view of the whole temple.

The Mahayana Hall is 36.75 metres high, the tallest wooden structure of its kind in China. It has six layers of eaves in front, four in the rear and five on the sides, and is actually three storeys high. On the roof are five square pavilions with gilded tiles. The interior has a series of galleries looking over a central well, which is occupied by a gigantic statue of Guanyin of a Thousand Arms and Eyes, with two companions, Sudhana and the Naga Maiden. Despite its name, the statue actually has only forty-two arms, a conventional way of representing one thousand. It is 22.28 metres high and weighs over 120 tons. On its head stands a statue of Amitabha, Guanyin's teacher; 1.2 metres high, it is nevertheless barely visible from the ground because of the great height of Guanyin. In her hands, Guanyin holds the sun,

the moon, a ribbon called the *hada* symbolizing the earth
and the heaven, a bell and a *vadjra* (mace). It is the
largest wooden statue of its kind in the world. Despite
its size, it is beautifully carved and proportioned, with
fine attention to detail — a masterpiece of Chinese sculpture. The two side statues are 16 metres high. Around
the side walls are the Ten Thousand Buddha niches (actually ten thousand and ninety); each niche is about
ten centimetres high and contains a gilded seated
Buddha. Along the galleries and at the back of the hall
are eight small Tibetan-style wooden pagodas and five
wooden images of Amitayus, each representing a different Buddhist story.

To the southeast of the Mahayana Hall beyond the
"continents" is a small courtyard where the Qianlong
emperor would rest on his visits to the temple; to the
southwest is another courtyard where lectures on the
scriptures were given.

To the east of the Puningsi stood the Puyousi (Temple of Universal Protection), now destroyed. It was built
in Chinese style but contained Tibetan images.

The Pulesi (Temple of Universal Joy)

The suppression of the Zungar rebellions helped
stabilize China's northwestern border areas. Afterwards, the chiefs of the Kazak[1] and Kirgiz[2] tribes from
Chinese Turkestan paid regular formal visits to Qianlong in Chengde. To show respect for their religious
beliefs as well as to strengthen control over the border
areas, Qianlong ordered the building of Pulesi in 1766
for their use. No lamas were in residence; instead the

[1]哈萨克；[2]柯尔克孜。

temple was administered by the Imperial Household Bureau.

Pulesi lies to the south of the Puningsi, on the east bank of the Wulie River. It is similar in layout to the Puningsi, except that it lies along an east-west axis, following the contours of its steep hill site. Now surrounded by vegetable gardens, it has a tranquil, rural air. The first courtyard has a front gate, drum and bell towers, and a devaraja hall with three glazed Tibetan-style pagodas on the roof ridge.

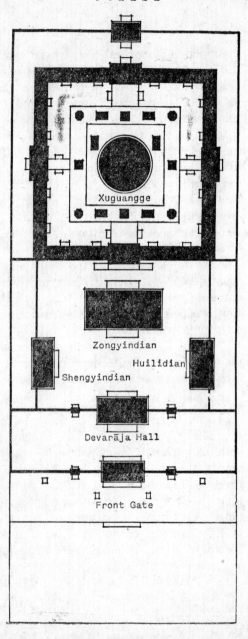

In the second courtyard is the main hall, the Zong-yindian (Hall of Manifest Faith) and two side halls, the Huilidian (Hall of the Power of Wisdom) and the Shengyindian (Hall of the Source of Victory). The rear section consists of a huge square platform which is entered through a stele pavilion. The platform is known as a *ducheng* (tower wall) and represents a *mandala*; it is elaborately carved with images of saints and Buddhas. This *mandala* platform supports a smaller two-tiered square platform with yellow tiled eaves and a white stone balustrade. On top of this platform is a circular building called the Xuguangge (Hall of the Dawn Light). The hall and its platform represent heaven and earth, which in Buddhist cosmology are respectively round and square. Inside the hall is another platform with a *mandala* made of thirty-seven pieces of wood, representing Sakyamuni's learning in thirty-seven fields. The image of the Lewangfo or Huanxifo (Laughing Buddha) is enshrined in the centre. The caisson ceiling has a dragon and phoenix design skilfully carved out of wood and covered with gold foil. On the lower tier of the platform are eight Tibetan-style pagodas, four at the corners and four at the centres of the four sides. The corner pagodas are white with a yellow glazed-tile decoration. Going counter-clockwise from the front pagoda (south), the remaining four are purple, black, green and white.

North of the Pulesi is the Anyuanmiao (Temple for the Pacification of Distant Regions), of which only the foundations, a few walls, an iron incense burner and the main hall still remain. It was built in 1764, on the model of a temple in the Ili valley in Xinjiang.

To the south of the Pulesi were the two Kangxi

temples, the Purensi (Temple of Universal Benevolence), also known as the Front Temple, and the Pushansi (Temple of Universal Kindness), also known as the Rear Temple. Both were built in 1713 in Chinese style, but the former is now in poor condition and the latter is no longer in existence.

The Putuozongchengmiao (Temple of the Potarak Doctrine)

North of the Hill Station on the hillside overlooking Shizigou (Lion Gully) is the second group of temples, of which the most impressive is the Putuozongchengmiao. The year 1770 was the sixtieth birthday of Qianlong and 1771 was his mother's eightieth year. To celebrate these auspicious events, the Qing court received visits at Chengde from a great number of Uygur and Mongolian tribes from the north and northwest. In honour of his visitors and to strengthen the ties between them, Qianlong ordered the construction of a lamasery built on the model of the Potala in Lhasa,[2] the centre of Lamaism. It took from 1767 to 1771 to complete. Just as work was being finished, the Torguts,[1] a Mongol tribe who had migrated to the banks of the Volga, returned to their homeland to escape Russian oppression. Qianlong held a ceremony at the main hall of the temple to celebrate their return.

The Putuozongchengmiao is by far the largest of the Chengde temples, covering 220,000 square metres. "Putuo" is a Chinese transcription of the Tibetan word *potala*, the name of a hill near Lhasa where the Dalai Lama's palace is situated, and used to refer to the palace; "Zongcheng" means "honoured city". Potala is also rendered in Chinese as "Pudala". The Putuozongcheng is

[1]土尔扈特；[2]拉萨。

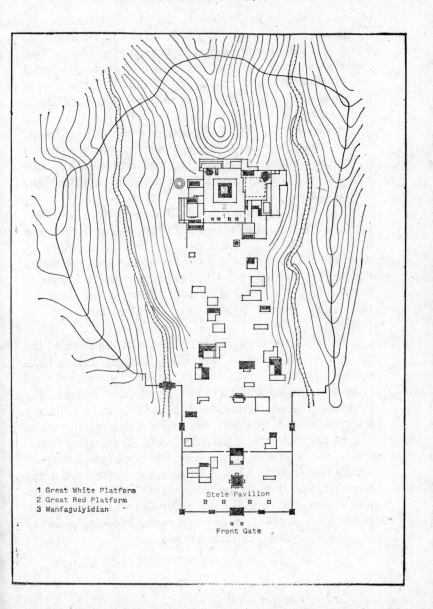

1 Great White Platform
2 Great Red Platform
3 Wanfaguiyidian

Stele Pavilion

Front Gate

often referred to in English as the "Little Potala".

The original access to the temple was via a bridge across a moat which is now a vegetable garden. Two stone lions guard the front gate which opens into a paved courtyard with a stele pavilion. This part of the temple is in Chinese style. Behind is the Five Pagoda Gate, a whitewashed Tibetan-style building with red false windows, surmounted by five pagodas each of a different colour. Two finely carved elephants in front are shaded by ancient pines. The five pagodas represent the five schools of Buddhism, and the elephants represent the Mahayana school.

The formal symmetry of Chinese temple architecture is at this point abandoned, though there continues to be a north-south orientation of the main buildings. A winding path follows the contours of the steeply-sloping site up to an elaborate Chinese-style memorial arch in green and yellow glazed tiles. In front of the arch are two stone lions, representing secular authority in Buddhism.

Between the arch and the Great Red Platform at the summit is an irregular series of Tibetan-style whitewashed platform buildings in various shapes, several storeys high and solid within. From front to back, the first has five white dagobas, the second has a Chinese-style wooden bell-tower, the third has a single white dagoba and others just have flat roofs. A platform building to the west has an attached Chinese-style courtyard which now houses some of the arhat statues from the former Luohantang. The informal layout of these buildings amongst the trees, grass and rocks creates a natural, peaceful atmosphere, in contract to the imposing presence of the Great Red Platform behind.

Towering over the buildings below, the Great Red Platform stands 43 metres high, and is modelled after the Red Palace of the Lhasa Potala. The six-storeyed red upper structure rests on a white stone base three storeys high, decorated with red false windows. In the centre of the facade of the upper platform is a vertical row of six glazed Buddhist niches, representing the six decades of Qianlong's life. Hidden from view within the high red walls of the platform is the main hall, the Wanfaguiyidian (Hall of All Laws Belonging to One). Formerly it was ringed by variously shaped three-storeyed buildings which have now been destroyed. The Wanfaguiyidian was the scene of religious ceremonies to celebrate the birthday of Qianlong's mother and it was also here that Qianlong received the Torgut chief. Formerly a picture of Amitayus embroidered with gold thread used to hang here, but it was stolen by the warlord Tang Yulin.[1] Now there are two "longevity pagodas" on either side of the altar, made of red sandalwood with ten thousand characters for "longevity" carved on them. One is in poor condition. The bodhisattva statues around the walls were brought in from elsewhere.

The Xumifushoumiao (Temple of Sumeru Happiness and Longevity)

A close neighbour to the east of the Putuozongchengmiao, the Xumifushoumiao is similar in structure and only slightly less imposing in size.

On Qianlong's seventieth birthday in 1780, the Sixth Panchen Erdeni came in person to Chengde to offer his congratulations. In honour of his visit, Qianlong ordered the construction of this temple after the model of the Panchen's lamasery in Tibet, the Trashi Lhümpo, to

[1] 汤玉麟。

serve as his residence. "Xumifushou" is the Chinese translation of Trashi Lhümpo: *trashi* means *fushou* (auspicious longevity), and *lhümpo* and *xumi* are both transcriptions of the Sanskrit *sumeru*, which literally means "mountain of marvellous height".

The temple played an important role in strengthening ties between the central government and Tibet. The blend of Chinese and Tibetan styles is much more advanced here than in the Putuozongchengmiao, showing the progress made in cultural interchange during the intervening decade. For example, the layout along the north-south axis is more symmetrical, with the Great Red Platform in the centre of the grounds and the pagoda at the rear, but in Tibetan style it follows more closely the contours of the hill site.

An arched bridge leads to the front gate, behind which is the Chinese-style courtyard with a stele pavilion. The central stele rests on a turtle base. Beyond is an elaborate archway with green and yellow glazed tiles, like the Putuozongchengmiao arch, and with two stone elephants in front.

North of the arch is the temple's main structure, the Great Red Platform, consisting of three storeys set on a high base. On each corner of the platform walls stands a corner tower. Semi-concealed within the platform walls is the main hall, the Miaogaozhuangyandian (Solemn Sumeru Hall), which is entered from the ground floor of the red platform. It was the place where the Panchen delivered his sermons. The double-roofed exterior of the hall is particularly splendid, with its gilded tiles and fish-scale ridges; along the four wave-shaped ridges are eight gilded imperial (five-clawed) dragons, backs arched and tails raised as if ready to spring. In-

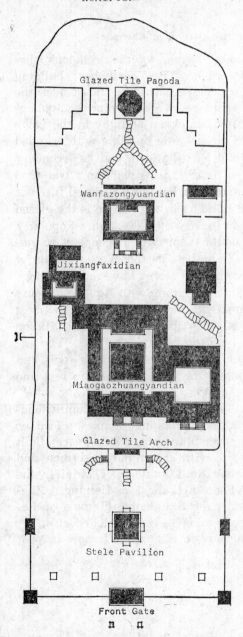

Glazed Tile Pagoda

Wanfazongyuandian

Jixiangfaxidian

Miaogaozhuangyandian

Glazed Tile Arch

Stele Pavilion

Front Gate

side the hall a statue of Tsong-khapa, the founder of the Yellow Sect, stands before Sakyamuni on the altar. The former thousand niches and murals have disappeared. Three-storeyed galleries along the inner wall of the platform enclose the hall in a deep courtyard.

Adjoining the southeast and northwest corners of the Great Red Platform are two smaller platform buildings, each two storeys high and both with access to the main hall in the inner courtyard. The southeast building, known as the East Red Platform, was a place for the emperor to

rest on his visits and listen to the religious dis-
courses of the Panchen. The northwest building
was the Panchen's residence, with fine views over the
dragon roof and the valley below. Known as the Jixiangfaxidian (Hall of Auspicious Omen and Joy in the Law),
it is a two-storeyed Chinese-style building with a gilded
roof. Behind the Great Red Platform and its secondary
buildings is a terraced courtyard, its walls in a bad state
of repair, with a two-storeyed hall with a glazed tile roof
at the rear. The last building in the temple is the glazed
tile octagonal pagoda, seven storeys high. Popularly
known as the Wanshouta (Longevity Pagoda), it resembles the pagoda at Xiangshan in the Western Hills of
Beijing. The walls on the first storey have relief carvings
of Buddhas on each side, beginning with Amitayus facing
south. From the pagoda one can enjoy perhaps the most
spectacular view of all, over the valley, the Hill Station
and the eastern and northern outer temples. The secluded setting high up the hill, the gleaming roofs and
the fragrant pines make this an ideal spot to rest and
refresh one's spirits.

West of the Putuozongchengmiao and Xumifushoumiao are the sites of the remaining temples. Two no
longer exist, the Guang'ansi (Temple of Vast Peace), built
in 1772 in Tibetan style with an ordination terrace, and
the Luohantang (Arhat Hall), built in 1774 after the
Anguosi (Temple of Peaceful Lands) in Haining,[1] Zhejiang. A third temple, the Shuxiangsi (Temple of Remarkable Images), built in 1774, was modelled after the
Shuxiangsi on Wutaishan[2] in Shanxi; it is now in poor
condition.

[1]海宁；[2]五台山。

5

Imperial Parks and Gardens

Apart from its magnificent collection of buildings, Beijing also enjoys the legacy of several famous imperial parks and gardens. Those which have survived into the present have now been turned into public parks which, together with the new parks created since Liberation, greatly enrich the beauty of the city and its outskirts. The most famous of all is the Yiheyuan, known to the world as the Summer Palace.

The Yiheyuan (Park of Nurtured Harmony)

This former imperial park in the northwestern outskirts of Beijing occupies 290 hectares, three-fourths of it water. The Chinese name means Park of Nurtured Harmony, but it is generally known to foreigners as the Summer Palace, just as Beihai Park around the Forbidden City was known as the Winter Palace. Its main features are Wanshoushan (Longevity Hill) and Kunminghu (Kunming Lake); in the distance can be seen the peaks of the Western Hills and the pagoda on Yuquanshan (Jade Spring Hill). The park's natural beauty is set off by a multitude of highly decorative halls, towers, galleries, pavilions, kiosks and bridges. Especially noteworthy is the ingenious way in which the architects adapted the buildings to blend in with or accentuate the natural surroundings, abandoning the formal courtyard style of the Forbidden City.

The history of the Yiheyuan goes back to the Yuan dynasty. Wanshoushan was then called Wengshan (Jar Hill) and Kunming Lake was Wengshanpo (Jar Hill Pond). The Yuan hydraulic engineer Guo Shoujing introduced spring water from Changping and Yuquanshan, north of Wengshan, to expand the pond into a large reservoir called Xihu (West Lake).

In the Qing dynasty, the natural protection offered by the Western Hills was put to good use by the construction of a vast area of pleasure grounds known as the "three hills and five parks": Changchunyuan (Park of Everlasting Spring) and Yuanmingyuan (Park of Perfection and Brightness); Jingmingyuan[1] (Park of Tranquillity and Brightness) at Yuquanshan; Jingyiyuan[2] (Park of Tranquillity and Pleasure) at Xiangshan (Fragrance Hill); and Qingyiyuan[3] (Park of Clear Ripples) at Wanshoushan, predecessor of the Yiheyuan. 1751 was the year of the 60th birthday of Madame Niugulu,[4] the mother of the fourth Qing emperor Qianlong. Construction projects to celebrate the occasion began a year earlier, centring on the Dabaoen Yanshousi (Temple of Gratitude for Longevity) at Xihu. Wengshan was renamed Wanshoushan, and Xihu became Kunminghu after a famous lake in the old Tang capital of Chang'an. The whole park was enclosed and renamed Qingyiyuan. It took fifteen years to finish and cost 4.8 million taels of silver. Its completion in 1764 was the last stage in the construction of the "three hills and five parks". From the Chang-

静明园；[2]静宜园；[3]清漪园；[4]钮祜绿。

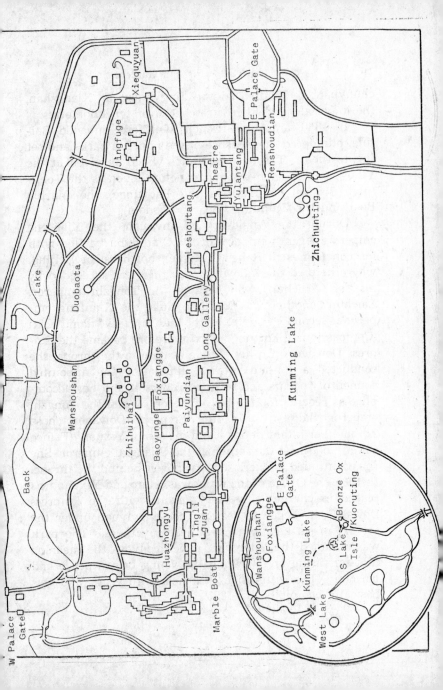

chunyuan at Haidian to the Jingyiyuan at Xiangshan, the imperial parks then stretched over ten kilometres.

In 1860, an Anglo-French joint force invaded Beijing, plundered the treasure of the imperial parks and set fire to them. The only buildings which survived at the Yiheyuan were non-wooden structures such as the Tongting (Bronze Pavilion) in the Baoyunge, the Marble Boat and the Zhihuihai (Sea of Wisdom).

During the Anglo-French invasion, the Xianfeng emperor, seventh emperor of the Qing dynasty, fled with his concubines to Rehe (Chengde), northeast of Beijing, where he died the following year. He was succeeded by his son, Zaichun, who became the Tongzhi emperor. Zaichun's mother was Madame Nala, the Xianfeng emperor's secondary wife, with the courtesy name Cixi (Compassionate Fortune). Cixi therefore became the Empress Dowager. On her son's elevation to the throne, she conducted a coup d'état by eliminating the appointed council of regents and setting up herself and her accomplice as regents for the boy emperor. When the Tongzhi emperor died in 1874, the Empress Dowager chose Zaitian, her infant nephew and the son of Yixuan[1] (Prince Chun), to ascend the throne as the Guangxu emperor. She thus continued to exercise great power behind the throne. In 1885, the Office of the Navy was set up and Yixuan was placed in charge. To curry favour with the Empress Dowager, he began to restore the Qingyiyuan under the pretext of setting up a naval academy there. The park was renamed the Yiheyuan, which conveys the meaning that nurturing or educating the young brings peace and harmony. The restoration took nearly 10 years, and was basically completed by 1895,

[1]奕譞。

In 1889, the Empress Dowager resigned her regency and retired to the Yiheyuan. After the 1898 attempt at reform under the Guangxu emperor, however, she virtually imprisoned her nephew and resumed her autocratic rule. When the allied forces of the eight powers invaded Beijing in 1900, the Empress Dowager and the Guangxu emperor fled to Xi'an. The Yiheyuan was severely damaged once again. After the Empress Dowager returned from Xi'an, she allocated a great deal of money for further restorations to the Yiheyuan. Most of her later years were then spent at the Yiheyuan. It was now not only her summer resort and pleasure garden for birthday celebrations, but also the secondary imperial palace for the administration of both domestic and foreign affairs.

The Empress Dowager's life at the Yiheyuan was very extravagant. When she came here with the Guangxu emperor, the attendant eunuchs on horseback and members of the band alone amounted to more than twelve hundred people, and more than forty carriages formed the procession. The kitchens occupied eight big courtyards and more than 128 kitchen eunuchs prepared food just for her. On the day after her arrival at the Yiheyuan she would attend an opera at the theatre in the Deheyuan. Once over 500,000 taels of silver were spent on stage props. Her sixtieth birthday was on the tenth day of the tenth lunar month of 1894; the previous year, 5,400,000 taels of silver were drawn from the state treasury to prepare for this auspicious event. Just the marquee set up before the Renshoudian used some 227.5 kilometres of coloured silks.

The Yiheyuan was closed down by Longyu, Guangxu's empress, after the Empress Dowager died in 1908.

After the 1911 Revolution, the Articles of Favourable Treatment signed by the new republic stipulated that the Yiheyuan still belonged to the Qing imperial family, and was to serve as a residence for Puyi, the last Qing emperor, after a temporary period of continued residence in the Forbidden City. (In fact, the emperor was allowed to stay in the rear of the Forbidden City until 1924.) In 1914, the Yiheyuan was opened by the imperial family to the public for an entrance fee. In 1924, when Puyi was driven out of Beijing, it was turned into a public park. The ticket price, however, was very expensive, so that few could afford to enter. During this period, the park became very run down; the buildings became dilapidated and objects were stolen.

Since Liberation, the government has assured the continued upkeep of the buildings and gardens of the Yiheyuan. It now receives over four million visitors annually, both Chinese and foreign.

The main entrance into the Yiheyuan is through the Donggongmen (East Palace Gate). It leads directly into the courtyard in front of the Renshoudian (Hall of Benevolent Longevity), where affairs of state were conducted by the Empress Dowager and the Guangxu emperor. The courtyard is planted with pines and cypresses. In front of the steps leading to the hall are a huge rock, a pair of bronze lions and a bronze *qilin* on a stone *sumeru* pedestal formerly at the Yuanmingyuan (the *qilin* is a legendary beast with a dragon's head, lion's tail, deer's antlers, ox's hooves and a body covered with fish-scales). On the terrace are symmetrically arranged pairs of bronze cauldrons, dragons and phoenixes. The hall itself is seven bays wide and faces east, and is kept in its original condition. North and south of the Ren-

shoudian are side halls, and outside the courtyard are
waiting rooms for the officials on duty.   These rooms
are symmetrically arranged on either side of a central
axis from the Donggongmen to the Renshoudian.   Because the halls and rooms are not part of the formal imperial palace they are roofed with grey tiles instead of
imperial yellow glazed tiles. The surrounding courtyards
are planted with pines, cypresses and banks of flowers,
with lake rocks for additional effect.

The residential area is behind the Renshoudian, and
is composed of three large courtyards connected by a
winding gallery 50 or 60 bays long. The principal building is the Leshoutang (Hall of Joyful Longevity), the residence of the Empress Dowager.   It faces Kunming
Lake in front and overlooks Wanshoushan to the rear;
to the east is the theatre in the Deheyuan (Garden of
Moral Harmony), and to the west is the famous Long
Gallery.   The hall is splendidly furnished and decorated
with objects such as the Many-Jewelled Flower-Basket
set with pearls, agates and jadeite, and the Fish Table
(for raising fish) inlaid with rare woods and ivory.   To
the south of the Leshoutang, connected by a winding
path, is the Yulantang (Hall of Jade Billows), residence of
the Guangxu emperor.   Behind it, to the north, is the
Yiyunguan (Hall of Pleasing Rue), the residence of the
Guangxu's empress.   The three courtyards are planted
with rare and exotic flowers and trees, including the
famous Yulan magnolias in front of the Leshoutang. The
interiors of the Leshoutang and Yulantang have been
preserved as they were left by their last inhabitants,
with the original curtained beds in the bedrooms and the
thrones and tables in the sitting rooms.   The two side
halls to the Yulantang were blocked off by a brick wall,

on the orders of the Empress Dowager, to confine the Guangxu emperor to house-arrest after the failure of the 1898 constitutional reforms which he attempted to carry out against her wishes.

Northeast of the Renshoudian is the Deheyuan (Garden of Moral Harmony), in which are the Yiledian (Hall of Nurtured Joy) and the theatre. The Yiledian, from which the Empress Dowager watched the performances, has been left in its original condition. It contains over 200 rare and precious objects, such as four screens inlaid with jade in a design of flowers and birds in the four seasons. The three-storeyed theatre has a double roof with upturned eaves, and a red upper railing and green pillars surrounding the stage, which is open on three sides. Trapdoors in the ceiling and floor allow dramatic entrances and exits for supernatural beings. The theatre was built specially for the Empress Dowager on her sixtieth birthday, and its construction cost over 700,000 taels of silver. On either side of the stage are galleries from which members of the imperial family and high officials could enjoy the performances; an invitation was considered a mark of extreme "benevolence".

West of the residential area is the most scenic part of the Yiheyuan, with Wanshoushan, Kunming Lake and the back lakes.

The famous Long Gallery, a covered way along the north bank of the lake, is 728 metres long and has four octagonal pavilions with double roofs at regular intervals. Each of its beams is painted with a scene from West Lake at Hangzhou, landscapes, human figures, battle scenes, flowers, birds and so on, so that it resembles an art gallery.

The broad expanse of Kunming Lake is embellished

with an island to the southeast, connected to the east bank with the Seventeen-Arch Bridge, 150 metres long and hanging like a rainbow across the water. To the west is a long causeway, like the Su Dongpo Causeway at West Lake; among its six bridges is the graceful fully-bowed Yudaiqiao (Jade Belt Bridge), which is supposed to look from a distance like a jade belt.

The southern slopes of Wanshoushan look down on the Long Gallery and the lake. In the centre at the lakeside is an elaborate arch, called the Yunhuiyuyu (Universe of Jade), from which a path leads north along an axis of splendid halls and towers. First are the Paiyunmen (Cloud Dispelling Gate), the Ergongmen (Second Palace Gate) and the Paiyundian (Cloud Dispelling Hall). The Paiyundian is the most important building on the axis. It was here that the Empress Dowager used to celebrate her birthday, and most of the objects on display are gifts from high officials on her seventieth birthday in 1905. A large oil-painting of the Empress Dowager was presented to her by the American painter Hubert Vos to celebrate her 71st birthday. Further north is the Dehuidian (Hall of Moral Brilliance), and behind on a huge stone plinth is the Foxiangge (Tower of Buddhist Incense), a three-storeyed building at the centre of the halls and towers, which can be seen from miles away. On the summit of the hill is the glazed-tile Zhihuihai (Sea of Wisdom) Tower. To the east of the Foxiangge are the Zhuanluncang (Cakravarti Tower), formerly a library for Buddhist scriptures, and a stele 9.88 metres high marking Wanshoushan and Kunming Lake. To the west are the Wufangge (Pentagonal Pavilion) and the Baoyunge (Precious Cloud Pavilion), a kiosk made entirely of bronze standing on a carved white marble *sumeru* pedestal. From the outside it appears to be made of wood painted with the green patina of bronze. It weighs 202,000 kilogrammes. A wall encloses the Baoyunge, Foxiangge, Zhuanlunge and Dehuidian. Further to the west is the Tingliguan (Hall for Listening to the Orioles), a former theatre now converted into a restaurant.

Further west again is the famous Marble Boat, formally known as the Qingyanfang (Boat for Pure Banquets). It has two decks built from large stone blocks, stained glass windows and elaborately carved marble facings. North of the boat is the Xingqiao (Water-Weed Bridge), followed by the Wanzihe (Srivatsa River) and the Banbiqiao (Hall-wall Bridge), leading to the back lakes to the north of Wanshoushan.

The back lakes and northern slopes of Wanshoushan form an area of natural scenery reminiscent of south-central China. The area was devastated by the imperialist invasions of 1860 and 1900, and most of the buildings are still in ruins. Some reconstruction has taken place since Liberation. Overlooking the north entrance is massive complex of buildings forming a Tibetan-style temple similar to the Puningsi and Pulesi at Chengde, called the Xiangyanzongyinzhige (Tower of Fragrant Rock and Manifest Faith). To the east is the Duobaota (Pagoda of Many Treasures) decorated with multi-coloured glazed tiles; further beyond is the Tiaoyuanzhai (Studio of Distant Views) and the Xiequyuan (Garden of Harmonious Interests). The Tiaoyuanzhai is built on an elevation which overlooks the roads outside the Yiheyuan walls. The Empress Dowager is said to have come here on the eighth day of the fourth month of the lunar calendar every year to watch the common people go to

the market at Miaofengshan (Mystic Peak Mountain), so
that it was given the name of Kanhuilou (Tower for
Watching the Fair). The Xiequyuan was built in imita-
tion of the Jichangyuan (Pleasure Garden) in Wuxi,
Jiangsu, during the Qianlong reign, and has been
called "the garden of gardens". There is a lotus-covered
pond which is surrounded by a long gallery with a
hundred bays, connecting thirteen towers and pavilions.
Rising in the centre of the pond is the Yinlushuixie
(Waterside Kiosk for Green Refreshment) where it is
said that the Empress Dowager used to come fishing.

Beihai (North Lake) Park and the Tuancheng (Round City)

Beihai Park, the former Winter Palace of Beijing's
emperors, is intimately bound up with the history of
Beijing. Originally this site was a swamp. Early in the
10th century, the Liao dynasty had built up an island
out of the swamp, called Yaoyu (Jade Islet), and a secondary imperial palace. In the 12th century, the Jin
dynasty drove out the Liao and took over its capital; they
renamed it Zhongdu (Central Capital) and built an imperial palace. A lake was dug in the present Beihai
area, and Qionghuadao (Jade Flowery Island) was built
up with an artificial hill made of lake rocks brought
from the lake region in south-central China. It is thought
that Qionghuadao was probably on the same site as
Yaoyu, and the Jin secondary palace on the island, the
Guanghandian (Hall of Vast Cold), may have been an
enlargement of the Liao palace. The Tuancheng was also
formed out of the lake at this time. In 1264 the Yuan
dynasty established its capital to the northwest of the

ruins of Zhongdu and named it Dadu (Great Capital).
Qionghuadao became the centre of Dadu, and remains
in the heart of modern Beijing. It was rebuilt three
times during the Yuan, and many palace buildings and
gardens were constructed then.

The big jade bowl in the Tuancheng and the Tieyingbi (Iron Shadow Screen) on the north bank of Beihai are
legacies from the Yuan. The Ming dynasty saw more
construction and renovation; the Wulongting (Five
Dragon-Pavilions) and Jiulongbi (Nine-Dragon Screen)
on the north bank of Beihai, and many halls, pavilions
and galleries on the Tuancheng all date from the Ming.

The largest-scale construction and restoration around
Beihai was carried out under the Qing. The Qing court
followed the layout of the Ming palaces and gardens. In
the eighth year of the Shunzhi reign (1651) a white tower
in Tibetan style, the Baita (White Dagoba), was erected
on the ruins of the Guanghandian, which had collapsed
almost 80 years earlier. In front of the dagoba a temple was built, which is now known as the Yong'ansi
(Temple of Eternal Peace). Further construction lasting
30 years took place during the Qianlong reign. The Wan-
folou (Tower of Ten Thousand Buddhas) was built at this
time in celebration of the 80th birthday of Qianlong's
mother. The three-storey tower contained 10,000 niches,
each holding a gilded Amitayus Buddha. When the allied
forces of the eight powers invaded Beijing in 1900, they
plundered all of its 10,000 Buddhas. When construction
was completed, Qianlong wrote inscriptions for four
steles, one for each side of the hill on which the Baita
stands, describing the scenery of Qionghuadao and the
history of its buildings. Beihai Park at present still
looks much as it did during the Qianlong reign.

BEIHAI PARK AND THE TUANCHENG

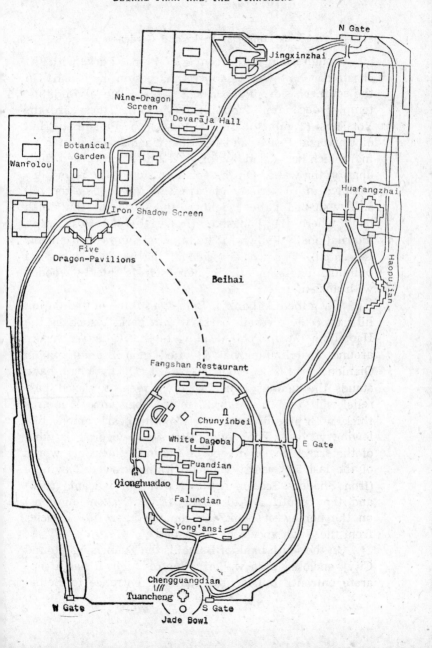

Qionghuadao is the centre of Beihai Park, with the chaste dagoba towering above the trees on the island. On the southern side of the island are a group of Buddhist temples decending the hillside; in order these are the Yong'ansi (Temple of Eternal Peace), the Pu'andian (Hall of Universal Peace) and the Shanyingdian (Hall of Karma) which has a cladding of glazed tiles and carved Buddhas on the walls. On the northern side of the island is a complex of rockeries and caves. At the foot of the hill a bow-shaped gallery follows the curve of the north bank where the Fangshan (Imperial-style) Restaurant, internationally known for its imperial Qing court cuisine, is located. The western side of the island has several buildings on it and the eastern side is thickly wooded with ancient trees.

Along the east bank of Beihai, a stretch of undulating hills conceals several "parks within parks", such as the Haopujian (Moat Pool), leading to the walled enclosure around the Huafangzhai (Painted Boat Studio), which Qianlong used as a secondary palace. On the north bank stands the famous Nine-Dragon Screen, a glazed bas-relief wall 5 metres high, 27 metres long and 1.2 metres thick, with nine dragons sporting with pearls among billowing waves. The vivid colours and vigorous styling of the screen makes it one of Beijing's finest art works of the last 500 years. The intricately carved Tieyingbi (Iron Shadow Screen, actually made of volcanic rock) and the beautiful Wulongting (Five Dragon-Pavilions) on the northwest bank, are among other fine legacies from the Yuan and Ming dynasties.

On the south bank of Beihai is the Tuancheng (Round City), enclosed by a wall five metres high; it has a separate entrance outside the southern entrance to Beihai

Park. The Tuancheng was originally an island formed
from the lake excavations in the 12th century, and its
purpose was to afford the court a fine view of the lake
and gardens. It now has an area of 4,500 square metres. An 800-year-old white pine still flourishes in the
courtyard.

The major building in the Tuancheng is the Cheng-
guangdian (Hall to Receive the Light) built in the Yuan
dynasty and repaired twice during the Ming and Qing.
Within the hall is a statue of Buddha, 1.5 metres high,
carved from a single piece of lustrous white jade. The
head and clothes are inlaid with red and green precious
stones. The jade Buddha is said to have come from
Burma in the Guangxu reign of the Qing dynasty. The
knife scar on its left arm was made by the allied forces
of the eight powers in 1900.

In the middle of the Tuancheng is the Yuwengting
(Jade Bowl Pavilion), with a blue roof and white columns.
The jade bowl inside, 0.66 metre in height and 1.5 metres in diametre, was used as a wine vessel by Kublai
Khan of the Yuan dynasty. It is carved out of a single
piece of black jade; on the outer surface are depicted
sea-dragons and other marine beasts disporting themselves in the waves, and inside is inscribed a poem about
the bowl by Qianlong. Originally the bowl was kept
in the Guanghandian on Qionghuadao. After the hall collapsed in the Ming dynasty, it was taken to the Zhen-
wumiao (True Martial Temple) at Xihuamen (West
Flowery Gate), the southwest entrance to the Forbidden
City, where it was used by Taoist priests as a pickle jar.
It was recovered in 1749 and this pavilion was built
especially for it on the orders of Qianlong.

Jingshan (Prospect Hill) Park

Jingshan Park is located on the meridian line north of the Palace Museum.

The park takes its name from Jingshan Hill, an artificial prominence covered with pines and cypresses which was originally part of the Imperial City, forming a protective screen to the palace. When the Yuan dynasty established its capital Dadu here, it was a small grassy hillock called Qingshan (Green Hill). When the city was rebuilt in the early years of the Ming dynasty, the earth excavated to make the moat around the Forbidden City was piled onto the hillock, forming the five peaks which can be seen today. Because coal was once heaped around the foot of the hill, it is also called Meishan (Coal Hill). In the Qianlong reign, fruit trees were planted and the grounds stocked with birds and animals; it was then known as the Baiguoyuan (Park of a Hundred Fruit Trees). At the same time, a pavilion was built on top of each of the five peaks as a place to rest and enjoy the scenery. From east to west, they are the Guanmiaoting (Wonderful View Pavilion), Zhouchangting (Surrounding View Pavilion), Wanchunting (Ten Thousand Springs Pavilion), Fulanting (Panoramic View Pavilion) and Jifangting (Harmonious Fragrance Pavilion). The topmost pavilion, Wanchunting, was the highest point within Beijing during the Qing dynasty. Formerly each of the pavilions contained a bronze statue of a god, which were collectively known as the Wuweishen (Five Flavour Gods). In 1900 four of them were stolen by the allied forces of the eight powers.

JINGSHAN PARK

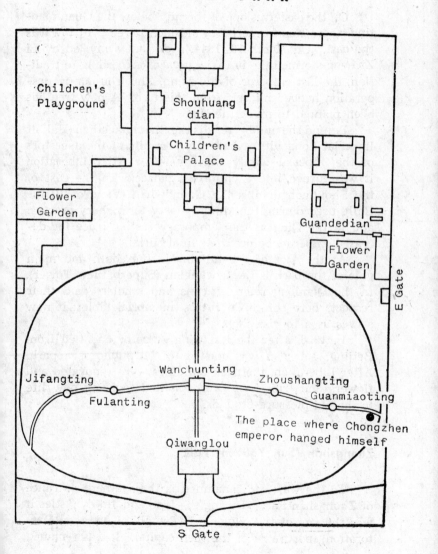

On the eastern slope of the hill, below the Guanmiaoting, there was formerly an old locust tree bent towards
the east. On March 19, 1644, a peasant army led by Li
Zicheng stormed the imperial palace. According to tradition, the last emperor of the Ming, Zhu Youjian, in des-
peration hanged himself from this tree. A new tree has
been planted to mark the site.

Behind the middle peak is the Shouhuangdian (Hall of
Imperial Longevity) where the portraits of the ancestors
of the imperial family were housed. After Liberation
it was turned into a children's palace. To the east of
the Shouhuangdian is the Guandedian (View of Virtue
Hall), used during the Ming dynasty for archery practice
and in the Qing as the temporary resting-place for deceased emperors before their final burial.

At the foot of the hill inside the south and main
gate of the park is the Qiwanglou (Superb View Tower).
In the Qianlong reign officials and scholars paid their
respects here before Confucius' memorial tablet; it now
serves as a tourist shop.

In 1928, after the last Qing emperor had fled from
Beijing, Jingshan was opened to the public as a park.
After Liberation, the park buildings were renovated and
flowers and fruit trees were planted to bring new life
to the old pleasure-grounds.

Zhongshan (Sun Yat-sen) Park

To the west of Tiananmen is the southern entrance
of Zhongshan Park. During the Liao and Jin dynasties it
was the site of the Xingguosi (Temple of National Restoration), northwest of the then capital. It was renamed

Wanshouxingguosi (Temple of Longevity and National Restoration) in the Yuan dynasty. When Yongle, the third emperor of the Ming dynasty, established the Ming capital here, he had the Shejitan (Altar of Land and Grain) built at this site, where sacrifices were offered to the God of Land and the God of Grain. In 1914 it was connected into a park, known as Zhongyang (Central) Park and opened to the public. In 1928, its present name was adopted in commemoration of Dr Sun Zhongshan[1] (Known to the West as Sun Yat-sen), leader of the 1911 Revolution.

The southern entrance opens onto a square surrounded on three sides by covered galleries. In the centre of the square is a memorial arch inscribed with the characters "Baowei Heping" (Safeguard Peace). Toward the end of the 19th century, the Yihetuan (Boxers) Movement arose in north China against the imperialist invaders. In 1900, Boxers killed Baron Von Kettler, the German minister to China, who had openly provoked them. The corrupt Qing government apologized to imperialist Germany for the incident and at Germany's demand built a memorial arch named after the minister at Dongzongbu *hutong* (lane) near Hademen (now Chongwenmen) in the old Legation Quarter. At the end of World War I in 1918, the conference of victorious nations decided to change the name to the Arch of the Triumph of Truth, and the following year it was moved into the park. Its present name was adopted in 1953 at a peace conference held in Beijing by representatives from Asian and Pacific countries. Guo Moruo,[2] the late

[1]孙中山; [2]郭沫若。

Chairman of the Chinese Committee for World Peace, wrote the inscription.

North of the square along an avenue running from east to west are seven ancient cypresses, said to have been planted during the Liao dynasty about one thousand years ago. The tree furthest to the east is joined by a locust tree which grows entwined with the cypress; this rare sight is known as "the embrace of the cypress and locust".

To the west of the square is the Lantingbeiting (Pavilion of the Orchid Pavilion Steles), originally one of the famous sights of the Yuanmingyuan called Lanting Bazhu (Eight Pillars of the Orchid Pavilion). After the destruction of the Yuanmingyuan, it was brought here in 1917. Examples of the calligraphy of great masters of the past are carved on the pavilion's eight columns, and a poem by Qianlong is inscribed on the back of the stele in his own handwriting.

Between the square and the pavilion is the hexagonal Xiliting (Pavilion of Practising Rites) with yellow tiles and vermilion lacquered doors and windows. It was formerly part of the Honglusi, the Ministry of Rites in the Ming and Qing dynasties. Before presenting themselves at court, officials coming to the capital to see the emperor for the first time had to practise the appropriate behaviour in this pavilion of the Honglusi. The pavilion was moved to the park in 1915.

Also in the southern part of the park are the Shuixie (Water Pavilion), a small island called Siyixuan (Year-Round Delight), the Tanghuawu (Greenhouse) where flowers are displayed all year round, and the famous goldfish tubs.

The main feature of the northern part of the park

ZHONGSHAN PARK

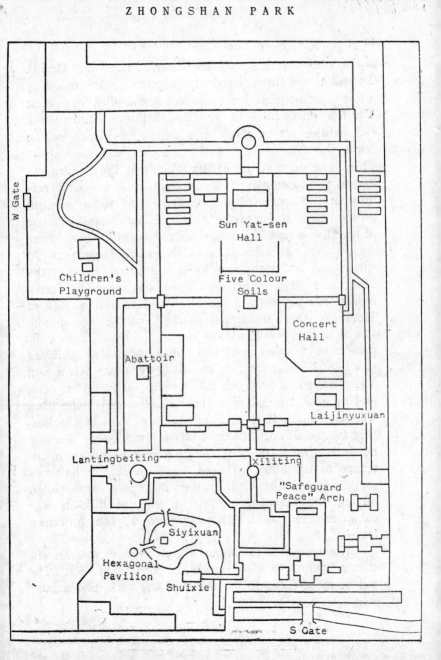

is the white marble Shejitan (Altar of Land and Grain). The altar is a three-tiered square terrace surrounded by a low glazed-tile wall in four colours and with four gates. The top tier is filled in with five different kinds of soil, red, white, black, green and yellow, sectioned off to mark the four points of the compass and the centre. This signified that the earth throughout the empire belonged to the emperor. There used to be a marble column in the centre of the terrace called the Shezhushi (Stone of the Ruler of the Earth) or Jiangshanshi (Stone of the Rivers and Mountains), signifying that state power was as firm and everlasting as rivers and mountains. On the second and eight months of the lunar calendar, the Ming and Qing emperors carried out sacrificial ceremonies here. North of the altar is the Baidian (Hall of Worship), where the emperors could rest; in case of rain, the ceremonies could also be performed here. This well-preserved wooden building dates back five hundred years to the beginning of the Ming dynasty. When Sun Yat-sen died in 1925, his coffin temporarily rested here, and in 1928, the hall was renamed Zhongshantang (Sun Yat-sen Hall). It is now the assembly hall of the Beijing People's Political Consultative Conference. Further north is Jimen (Halberd Gate), formerly the main entrance to the altar. It used to house 72 iron halberds for the protection of the altar, but these were stolen during the invasion of 1900 when the Baidian was commandeered as the headquarters of the American forces.

Northwest of the altar and its buildings is an entrance leading to Wumen and the Forbidden City. The palace moat flows to the north of the park, and a busy

children's playground is located in the northeastern
section.

The Working People's Palace of Culture

The Working People's Palace of Culture is entered
to the east of Tiananmen, on the site of the Taimiao
(Supreme Ancestral Temple) of the Ming and Qing
dynasties. The enclosed grounds are densely planted
with ancient cypresses, which occupy half of the whole
area. Cypresses were frequently planted around temples
to impart an air of solemnity.

The temple consists of three main buildings: the
temple proper, the middle hall and the rear hall. Built
in 1420, these three magnificent halls are very imposing.
In front is the Dajimen (Great Halberd Gate), five bays
wide. The 120 halberds formerly contained here were
plundered by foreign troops in 1900. South of the gate
are five small, exquisite bridges with white marble balustrades. Between the bridges and the gate are a number of buildings attached to the temple, such as a hexagonal pavilion over a well, a storehouse, kitchen, abat-
toir and curing-house.

In imperial days, the resident staff of the temple
consisted of several dozen court eunuchs, to tend the
memorial tablets, incense burners and candles. When
the emperor was enthroned, married, received prisoners
of war or returned triumphantly from battle, the temple
became a place of great bustling and excitement as the
emperor came to offer sacrifices to his ancestors.

The temple was converted into the Beijing Working
People's Palace of Culture in 1950. Later additions in-

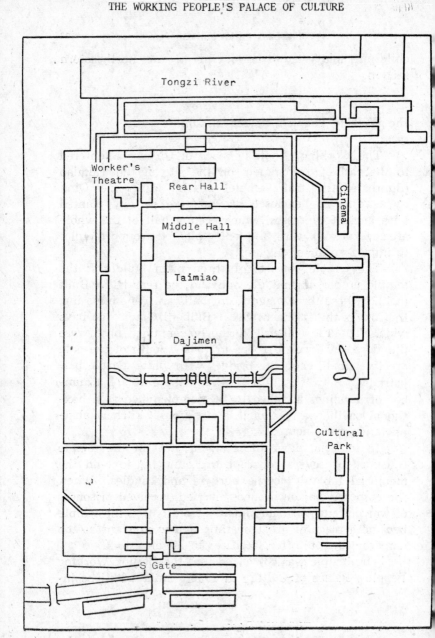

clude an open-air theatre, a well-lit basketball field, a cinema, chess and reading rooms and a children's playground. Exhibitions and lectures are now held in the old temple halls.

Tiantan (Altar of Heaven) Park

Located in the southern district of Beijing, Tiantan Park extends over an area of 270 hectares, triple the total area of the Palace Museum.

Its main buildings date back to 1420, when the third Ming emperor, Yongle, ordered the construction of an altar for the worship of heaven and earth. Later when the Fangzetan or Ditan (Altar of Land) was constructed for the worship of the earth, Tiantan was reserved for the worship of heaven and prayer for good harvests. Originally Tiantan was outside the walled city. In 1554, the southern suburbs were enclosed and became the "outer city". Since then, Tiantan has been part of the city proper.

Tiantan is the largest group of temple buildings in China and took fourteen years to complete. It is enclosed by a double wall, the upper or northern half of which is circular, representing heaven, and the lower or southern half square, representing earth; the combination of the two shapes indicates the original dual nature of Tiantan. The main temple buildings are clustered at the northern and southern ends of a long central causeway, 2.5 metres high and 360 metres long. The causeway is known as the Danbiqiao (Cinnabar Stairway Bridge) or Shendao (Sacred Way).

At the centre of the northern end is the main temple

hall, the Qiniandian (Hall of Prayer for Good Harvest), which has a history of over five hundred years. It was originally known as the Dasidian (Great Sacrificial Hall). During the Jiajing reign of the Ming dynasty, it was restored and renamed Daxiangdian (Great Offerings Hall), and its present name was bestowed during the Qing dynasty. In 1889 it was destroyed by lightning and restored to its original condition the following year. It was here that the emperor prayed in person for good harvests in the first lunar month of every year.

The hall is a circular wooden structure, 38 metres high and 30 metres in diameter. It has a triple conical roof set with deep blue glazed tiles and topped with a large gold-plating knob. The building stands on a three-tiered circular terrace called the Qigutan (Altar for Grain Prayers), which is a smaller version of the altar at the southern end of the causeway. In fact, the offering was not made on the terrace but inside the hall. Each tier of the terrace is edged with a white marble balustrade, and in the centre of each of four flights of steps up to the hall are white marble ramps carved with dragons, phoenixes and clouds. This superb temple on its marble terrace is a world-famous symbol of ancient Beijing, almost as well-known as Tiananmen itself.

The construction of the hall is a fine example of the unique methods of traditional Chinese architecture. Instead of iron nails, cement or reinforcing rods, the whole structure is supported by wooden mortise and tenon joints and wooden brackets on huge supporting pillars. There are altogether 28 pillars, of red-lacquered *nanmu* (a fine hardwood), symbolizing the 28 constellations. The four central pillars are the thickest, and are painted with gilded coiled dragons; they symbolize the

The Taihedian (Hall of Supreme Harmony), or Throne Hall, the biggest building in the Forbidden City, was the place where the emperor ascended the throne and celebrated important festivals.

The throne room of the Yangxindian (Hall of Mental Cultivation), where the emperor received high officials.

The carved stone ramp behind the Baohedian (Hall of Preserving Harmony), the largest in the Forbidden City.

Zhu Di (the Yongle emperor of the Ming dynasty), the first emperor to live in the Forbidden City.

Aisin-Gioro Puyi, the last emperor of the Qing dynasty and the last inhabitant of the Forbidden City.

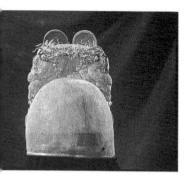

Imperial crown.

"The Great Qing Son of Heaven" seal, made of gilded silver (two views).

Phoenix crown (worn by empresses and imperial concubines).

The Yanbozhishuangdian (Hall of Refreshing Mists and Waves), the emperor's bedroom at the Chengde Hill Station.

The Jinshanting (Gold Hill Pavilion), in the grounds of the Hill Station.

Xumifushoumiao (Temple of Sumeru Happiness and Longevity).

The Mahayana Hall , the main building in the Puningsi (Temple of Universal Tranquillity).

The Guanyin of A Thousand Arms and Eyes in the Mahayana Hall of the Puningsi, the largest wooden image of a Buddha in China.

千手千眼觀世音菩薩木雕佛像

中国 承德

Jingshan (Prospect Hill) Park.

The Nine-dragon Screen in Beihai Park, with nine dragons sporting with pearls in billowing waves, dating from the Ming dynasty.

The Wanshoushan (Longevity Hill) in the Yiheyuan (Summer Palace), where the Empress Dowager Cixi of the Qing dynasty would come for recreation and birthday celebrations.

Tourists being photographed in traditional Chinese costume after a banquet at the Tingliguan (Hall for Listening to the Orioles) in the Summer Palace.

Giant panda
and her cub.

An autumn outing at the Great Wall.

TIANTAN PARK

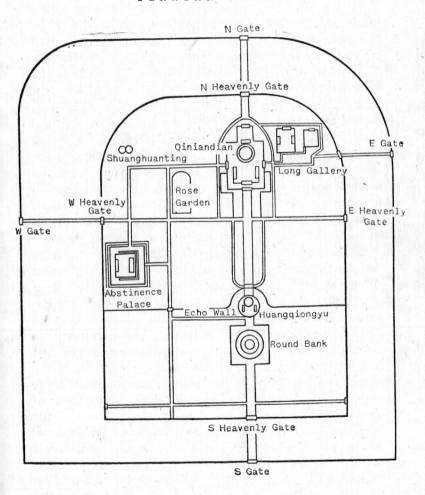

four seasons of the year. Around them is an inner circle of twelve pillars, symbolizing the twelve months of the lunar calendar, and beyond is an outer circle of another twelve, symbolizing the twelve two-hour periods into which the cycle of day and night was traditionally divided. The twenty-four pillars taken together represent the 24 solar periods of each year. (The solar year in the Chinese calendar was divided into twenty-four periods, named according to the typical weather and agricultural conditions of north China. The solar periods in spring are the beginning of spring, rain showers, awakening insects, spring equinox, clear brightness, grain rain; the solar periods in summer are the beginning of summer, full grain, grain in the ear, summer solstice, moderate heat, great heat; the solar periods in autumn are the beginning of autumn, reduced heat, white dew, autumn equinox, cold dew, descent of frost; the solar periods in winter are the beginning of winter, light snow, heavy snow, winter solstice, moderate cold, severe cold.)

Inside the hall is a coffered ceiling carved in a design of dragons and phoenixes. The floor is paved with flagstones and in the centre is a slab of marble with a natural veining resembling a dragon and phoenix design. The original furnishing of the hall is retained. In the centre is a long table, a throne and a screen, where there used to be placed the memorial tablets of the gods of heaven and earth. To the east are two screens, chairs and tables, where offerings were made to the imperial ancestors. To the west are a birchwood screen carved with landscapes, human figures, towers and pavilions, and a hardwood throne where the emperor rested after having performed the ceremonies. In front of the hall are an eight-diagram burner and a bronze tripod, several hundred years old.

South of the Qiniandian is the Qinianmen (Gate of Prayer for Good Harvest), dating from the Ming dynasty and still containing some Ming murals. From this gate stretches a square wall enclosing the Qiniandian and its auxiliary buildings. North of the wall is the Huang-qiandian (Hall of the Imperial Heaven), also a Ming building. To the east of the Qiniandian are the Qixingshi (Seven Star Stones), carved with cloud patterns; they were traditionally believed to be meteors, but are actually man-made objects symbolizing natural phenomena. There is also an intertwining locust and cypress tree here.

Towards the southern end of the causeway is a wall which cuts off the lower one-third of the grounds from the northern part. South of the wall is the Huangqiong-yu (Imperial Vault of Heaven), a single roofed circular structure with deep blue glazed tiles, like a smaller version of the Qiniandian. The building is 19.5 metres high and 15.6 metres in diameter. The roof is supported by eight eave pillars and eight golden pillars. The carved coffered ceiling is in three concentric tiers, a design rare in Chinese architecture. The function of the Huangqiong-yu was to house the memorial tablet of the "Supreme Ruler of Heaven".

Around the Huangqiongyu is the famous Echo Wall, built according to the principle that a sound wave bounces off a curved wall many times in succession. A whisper at one point of the wall can be heard clearly at an opposite point. In front of the steps at the southern entrance to the wall are the Three Echo Stones. A handclap over the first stone produces a single echo, a handclap on the second stone a double echo and a handclap on the third stone a triple echo. The disparity lies in the different distances the sound wave has to travel on its way back from the Echo Wall. North of the Echo Wall is the Nine-dragon Cypress, which is so knotted that it seems entwined by dragons. It is over 500 years old but still flourishes.

The Huanqiu (Circular Mound) is a three-tiered circular marble terrace south of the Huangqiongyu. It is enclosed by a double wall, the outer of which is square, the inner circular. Its formal name is the Huanqiutan (Circular Mound Altar). It has a maximum height of five metres, and the three tiers are respectively seven, five and three metres in diameter. Marble balustrades enclose each tier, and along the balustrades are altogether 360 balusters, symbolizing the number of degrees in a circle. Every year at the time of the winter solstice, the emperor came here personally to offer sacrifices to heaven. The "tablet of the god of heaven" would be taken from the Huangqiongyu for the ceremony and returned afterwards. Because heaven is round, the altar is round; because heaven is vast and open, the altar is open without any superstructural building. In the centre of the top tier is a circular flagstone surrounded by nine concentric circles of flagstones, forming the surface of the upper tier. The innermost circle is made up of nine blocks of stone and the outermost has 81. According to ancient Chinese cosmology, the sun is a manifestation of the *yang* (male) principle, and therefore the number of the various component parts of the altar must also be *yang*, that is, an odd number or a multiple of odd numbers. A whisper from the central stone on the top of the altar sounds louder to the speaker than to bystanders, because the sound waves spread in different directions quickly to the stone balustrades and surrounding walls and are immediately reflected back to the central spot.

The Huanqiu was built in 1530. Despite several earthquakes since the altar was built, its surface has remained extremely even and its stones fit closely.

Beijing Zoo

Located in the western outskirts of the city, the Beijing Zoological Garden is the oldest zoo in Chinese history and the biggest at the present time. During the Ming dynasty it was the site of an imperial park. In early Qing it became a private garden of an imperial relative, and in late Qing it was turned into an experimental farm on the orders of the Empress Dowager Cixi who had a small menagerie known as the Wanshengyuan (Garden of Ten Thousand Beasts) opened here for her personal enjoyment. It included tigers, leopards, lions, elephants, zebras, ostriches and other rare animals and birds, and was opened to the public in 1908. During the Japanese occupation of 1937-1945, most of the animals were destroyed. On the eve of Liberation it contained only a dozen or so monkeys, several parrots and an ostrich caught in Zhongshan Park.

The Zoo was reopened in 1950 as the southeastern part of the Western Suburbs Park. In 1955 the Zoo was expanded to cover the whole park and renamed the Beijing Zoological Garden. After 1956, special enclosures were built for hippopotamuses, rhinoceroses, elephants, antelopes, lions, tigers, giraffes and pandas. In 1973, enclosures for orang-outangs, chimpanzees, marine animals, amphibious animals and reptiles were also opened to the public. The Zoo now occupies an area of

50 hectares, five times its original size, and contains more than six thousand animals of over 550 species. Most of the animals are from different parts of China, but important species from each of the major continents are also represented.

A major attraction of the Zoo is its world famous giant panda house. The giant panda was originally a carnivore, but because of changes in its environment it now subsists chiefly on bamboo. Zoologists call the giant panda "a living fossil" for it still has some of the morphological and structural characteristics of ancient mammals. An adult giant panda weighs over 100 kilogrammes but a newborn cub is very tiny and weighs only 150-200 grams. It has white body hair with black hair on its paws and ears and around its eyes.

Another rare animal native to China is the Milu, or Père David's deer (Elaphurus davidianus). Original to northern China this aberrant member of the deer family has left fossilized remains in Japan, but nowhere exists in its natural state. Its tail is somewhat like a donkey's, its hooves are somewhat like an ox's, its neck is somewhat like a camel's and its antlers are somewhat like a deer's, and so the animal is known in Chinese as the "quadruple unlikeness".

The Zoo's birds inhabit the area around Yingchundao (Sea of Spring Island), the most scenic part of the Zoo. Its stock includes waterfowl, songbirds, wading birds, peacocks and golden pheasants. Furred animals such as beavers, sables, golden cats, leopard cats, marmots and foxes inhabit the "small zoo" east of the main entrance. Camels and Tibetan yaks can be found to the north and west of the entrance.

Other rare animals in the Beijing Zoo are presents

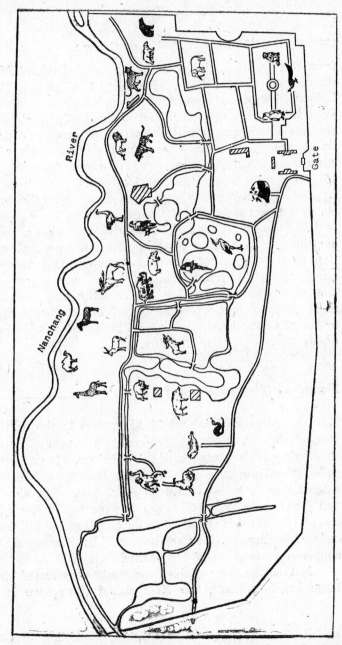

BEIJING ZOO

Nanchang River

Gate

from foreign countries, such as the small elephant Methura, given by the former Premier of Sri Lanka, Mrs Bandaranaike, and a musk ox donated by the former President of the United States, Richard Nixon. There are also polar bears from the North Pole, penguins from the South Pole, manatees from the Gulf of Mexico, cassowaries from Indonesia, white peacocks from India, elephants, zebras, giraffes, ostriches, lions and hyenas from Africa, kangaroos and emus from Australia and eagles and leopards from America.

The Beijing Zoo is an educational institution as well as a place of recreation. Each enclosure has an explanation of the occupants' habitat, behaviour and natural environment. Along the pathways are explanatory notices about the origin of life, the evolution and development of the species, which birds and animals are helpful or harmful to mankind, and which birds and animals are under state protection in China.

Xiangshan (Fragrance Hill) Park

Xiangshan Park, about 21 kilometres to the northwest of Beijing, is one of the most picturesque spots in the city's outskirts. On top of the hill are two huge rocks, called the Rufengshi (Breast Peak Rocks), which are shaped like incense-burning *ding* (tripods). The clouds and mist which frequently wreathe the top of the hill therefore seem like clouds of incense, and so the hill was called Xianglushan (Incense Burner Hill); Xiangshan is simply a contraction of that name.

In 1186 the ruler of the Jin dynasty constructed two large buildings here, the Xiangshansi (Fragrance Hill

Temple) and a summer palace. Later renovations and additions under the Yuan, Ming and Qing culminated with the transformation of the grounds into the Jingyi-yuan (Park of Tranquillity and Pleasure) in 1745 under Qianlong. A Yuan restoration cost 500,000 taels of silver, and a Ming restoration cost over 700,000 taels. Like the other great parks in the western outskirts such as the Yiheyuan and Yuanmingyuan, the Jingyiyuan was ravaged by invading foreign troops in 1860 and again in 1900. All that remained were a glazed-tile arch, a glazed-tile pagoda and a pair of bronze lions guarding the entrance. For many years the park lay in ruins. A large-scale restoration of the grounds and buildings took place after Liberation, when flowers and fruit trees transformed the park into a beautiful garden again. It is a particularly popular place in autumn when the maple leaves redden. Many of the buildings are now being restored, and a modern hotel designed by I. M. Pei is being erected.

Inside the northern entrance to the park is the Tibetan-style Zhaomiao (Luminous Temple), built in 1780 as a residence for the Sixth Panchen Erdeni of Tibet on his visits to Beijing. In front of the temple is glazed-tile memorial archway and to the west is the octagonal seven-storey Glazed-Tile Pagoda with 56 bronze bells dangling from its eaves. The temple buildings closely resemble the Xumifushoumiao in Chengde, which was also built at this time.

In the southeast corner of the park, below the ruins of the Xiangshansi, is a small pool fed by two springs, named Shuangqing (Twin Clear Waters). It is said that one day Emperor Zhangzong[1] of the Jin dynasty dreamed

[1]章宗,

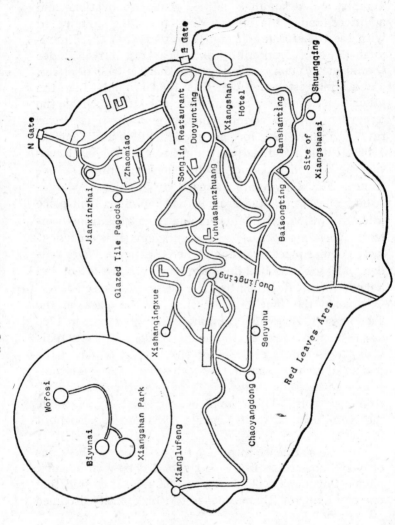

XIANGSHAN PARK

on a visit to Xiangshan that he shot an arrow which landed at a gushing spring. The next day he ordered that this spot be dug up, and springs were found. The Shuangqing springs are also known as the Mengganquan (Dream Springs). On the other side of the extensive Xiangshansi site is the Banshanting (Halfway Pavilion), which offers a splendid view of the valley. Keen climbers may continue to the peak along this or several other routes.

The Ruins of the Yuanmingyuan
(Park of Perfection and Brightness)

The Yuanmingyuan was one of the five great parks established during the Qing dynasty northwest of Beijing. Its construction employed armies of skilled builders and assembled the best building materials in the country over a period of 150 years. It is actually three separate parks. The earliest park, dating from the Yongzheng reign, was called the Yuanmingyuan and the two parks added later to the east and southeast under Qianlong were named the Changchunyuan (Park of Everlasting Spring) and Qichunyuan (Park of Superb Spring) which was later renamed Wanchunyuan (Park of Ten Thousand Springs). Since the three parks shared common borders they are generally referred to collectively as the Yuanmingyuan. Together they covered an area of over 300 hectares with a circumference of ten kilometres.

The Yuanmingyuan was located north of Haidian on the northwestern outskirts of the city. With the Western Hills nearby, rice fields and lotus ponds, it was a site of great natural beauty, and a number of artificial lakes, hills and valleys had added variety and charm to the natural landscape. The largest artificial lake was the Fuhai (Sea of Happiness) in the western part of the original Yuanmingyuan. Seemingly floating on its surface like a fairy isle was the Pengdao Yaotai (Fairy Isle and Jade Terrace). Inside the south and main gate, Dagongmen (Great Palace Gate), are the Qianhu (Front Lake) and Houhu (Back Lake), and around these two lakes are nine small islands symbolizing the nine states of ancient China.

Scattered over the vast expanse of lakes and hills were hundreds of painted and gilded palaces, halls, towers, pavilions and kiosks, some of which contained valuable art treasures and libraries. Five Qing emperors, from Yongzheng to Xianfeng, spent the greater part of the year at the Yuanmingyuan, holding audience and conducting the affairs of the empire. Inside the Dagongmen administrative offices corresponding to those in the Forbidden City were set up, as well as offices for the cabinet, ministries and military council. The Yuanmingyuan thus became the ruling centre of the feudal empire.

Because of its central importance, the Yuanmingyuan came to be a park of unprecedented size and grandeur. The landscaping was based on the famous gardens of south-central China, and the buildings embodied the most refined techniques of Chinese art and architecture. Its fame spread far and wide under the rubric of "park of parks", and it occupied an important place in the history of world gardens and parks.

In 1860, the Anglo-French joint force invaded Beijing. In order to punish the Qing emperor (who had fled to Chengde) for his intransigence, the commanders decided to destroy his favourite park. A few precious objects were reserved for Queen Victoria and Napoleon III, and then the troops were set free to plunder at will. Afterwards the whole grounds were set on fire. Even then, the destruction was not complete, and an attempt was made by the Empress Dowager Cixi to restore it in 1879. The project collapsed for lack of funds, but the place remained an imperial possession. In 1900 the remaining buildings were sacked again by the allied forces of the eight powers. After this second blow, the deterioration became more rapid. Warlords, bandits, officials, merchants and local hooligans stole or destroyed what was left, the ancient trees were cut down and even the building stones and lake rocks were carried off.

In one corner of the park the ruins are actually quite substantial and conspicuous. This is to the north of the Changchunyuan where a group of Western-style buildings once stood. Construction of these buildings was begun in 1745 after the design prepared by Jesuits employed at the Qing court, including Guiseppe Castiglione, Michel Benoist and Jean Denis Attiret. The foremen were also European Jesuits and the workmen were Chinese. The buildings were in Renaissance style and many were embellished with fountains and pools, but the roofs were covered with Chinese glazed tiles and inlaid five-colour glazed tiles were on the inside walls. Because they were constructed mainly of stone, much of basic structure survived the fires which destroyed the wooden Chinese buildings.

Some of the stone pieces that escaped destruction were moved to other places. The most well-known is the Lanting Bazhu (Eight Pillars of the Orchid Pavilion) which now occupies an important position in Zhongshan Park. The splendid marble *huabiao* standing in pairs in the courtyard of Beijing Library and in front of the main building at Beijing University come from the Anyougong (Palace of Blessed Peace) in the northwest corner of the Yuanmingyuan. The stone fish on the bank of the Weiminghu (Nameless Lake) at Beijing University was originally part of a fountain called Xieqiqu (Harmonious Interest) in the Changchunyuan. Five stone screens with carvings of army banners, armour, swords and artillery, which have now been returned to the Yuanmingyuan, were also at the university for many years.

Today scarcely anything is left even of the ruins or of the broad pathways except a few hardly discernible outlines of the park and some narrow, winding trails around the hills. Much of the area has been planted with trees since 1949 and peasants now till the fields around the lakes. It is an area of tranquil rural scenery, a pleasant place to stroll around and enjoy the fresh air and open spaces. The location of former beautiful spots can still be traced with the help of a map, and some idea of its former glory can be obtained.

Plans were made after Liberation to turn the Yuanmingyuan into a park and restore some of the ruins and gardens. In 1976, a Yuanmingyuan administration was set up and proceeded to clear the grounds and reassemble the scattered stone ruins of the European buildings. Paths and bridges were also repaired to allow access. A museum at the northeast entrance, near the European ruins, has an exhibition illustrating the history of the Yuanmingyuan and plans for its future.

6

The Imperial Tombs

The mountains around Beijing were chosen by most of the emperors of the last two feudal dynasties in China as auspicious sites for imperial burial grounds. Their tombs along with those of their consorts and daughters were concentrated in three areas, the Ming tombs to the northwest and the Qing tombs to the east and to the west.

The Ming Tombs

The Ming Tombs lie at the foot of the Tianshou Mountains, some 50 kilometres northwest of Beijing. Thirteen of the sixteen Ming emperors were buried here, so that the necropolis is known in Chinese as the Shisan-ling (Thirteen Tombs). These tombs are the best-preserved of all Chinese imperial tombs. Construction of the necropolis continued over 200 years, almost throughout the whole of the dynasty: construction of the first tomb, the Changling, began in 1409, and the last one, the Siling, was built in 1644 for the last emperor of the Ming dynasty by the first Qing emperor.

The Ming dynasty was founded in 1368 by Zhu

Yuanzhang, who made Nanjing his capital and was buried there after his death in 1398.

Zhu Di, fourth son of Zhu Yuanzhang, was enfeoffed when his father came to power as the Prince of Yan with his capital at the former Yuan capital of Dadu which was renamed Beiping (Northern Peace). After the first emperor died, his grandson Zhu Yunwen took the throne. Zhu Yunwen adopted measures to weaken the powers of his uncles, princes of large areas throughout the country. These measures met with resistance from Zhu Di, the most powerful of all the princes. In the name of "wiping out evil for the country", Zhu Di began an interfamilial war which lasted three years and ended with Zhu Di seizing Nanjing. In 1403 he proclaimed himself the third Ming emperor adopting the reign title Yongle. The burial site of the second emperor is unknown. In order to consolidate unity and strengthen his control over the whole country, the northern part in particular, the Yongle emperor moved his capital from Nanjing to Beiping, which was then renamed Beijing (Northern Capital). In 1406, he began building the Forbidden City, and the construction of his tomb started about the same time. In 1407 he ordered a search made for an "auspicious" burial site amid beautiful scenery in the vicinity of Beijing. It is said that Yongle was dissatisfied with the first choice, the Tanzhesi (Pool and Zhe Tree Temple) in western outskirts of Beijing, and so the present site was finally chosen. Undulating hills formed a natural protective screen to the north; the Dragon Hill and Tiger Hill stood like generals guarding the gateway to the south; the Wenyu River wound east towards the Great Hebei Plain from the Dongshan Pass in the southeast. Yongle was greatly pleased with the grandeur of this

Stone animals before the Ming Tombs, the burial ground of 13 Ming emperors, 50 km. northwest of Beijing.

Central Hall of the "Underground Palace", Dingling, tomb of the 13th Ming emperor. Shown here are the three marble thrones of the emperor and his two empresses.

Front view of the Western Qing Tombs at Yixian, Hebei.

Main hall of the Yu-ling, tomb of the Qianlong emperor at the Eastern Qing Tombs at Zunhua, Hebei.

Main Hall in the Yonghegong (Palace of Harmony and Peace), the biggest lamasery in Beijing

The 54-ton recumbent bronze Buddha in the Wofosi (Temple of the Recumbent Buddha), cast in the Yuan dynasty over 600 years ago.

The 46.5-ton big bell in the Juesheng Temple.

The Buddha's Tooth Pagoda in the Lingguang (Temple of Divine Light).

The ancient gingko tree at the Tanzhesi (Pool and Zhe Tree Temple), believed to have been planted 1,000 years ago and named "Emperor of Trees" by the Qianlong emperor of the Qing.

Beijing Muslims praying at the Dongsi Mosque.

Buddhist monks and laymen offering incense and reciting
Buddhist scriptures at the Guangjisi (Temple of Vast Succour).

Foreign and Chinese Catholics attending mass
at the Nantang (Southern Cathedral).

fertile valley. He conscripted peasants and artisans from Shandong, Shanxi, Henan and Zhejiang to carry out the construction, and army garrisons around Beijing were also ordered to help. Apart from the tomb itself, elaborate approaches and external buildings were planned, and the result was so impressive that all succeeding Ming emperors, with one exception, were buried here. (The seventh emperor was dethroned and buried in a modern tomb near Xiangshan.)

The present Ming tombs are spread over an area of more than 40 kilometres in circumference. A "Sacred Way", along which the bodies of the deceased emperors were reverently carried, stretches seven kilometres from south to north through the centre of the site. The Sacred Way begins at a huge marble archway, built in 1540 but still in excellent condition. It is 29 metres wide and supported by six marble pillars. The massive pedestals are decorated with relief carvings of dragons and clouds, and on top of each pedestal squats a stone animal. The carvings on the five arches are also very fine.

The Sacred Way leads first to the main gate, the Dagongmen (Great Palace Gate), which has three passageways with vermilion walls and a yellow glazed-tile roof. The central passageway was for the deceased emperor only; the living emperor used a side passage. There are tablets on each side of the gate inscribed with the words "Officials and others dismount here". The list of prohibitions relating to the Imperial Tombs decreed a whipping for anyone found collecting wood or breaking off twigs in the tombs area, execution for anyone found removing stones or soil, and a hundred beatings with a stick for anyone entering without official permission; anyone entering the area, whether official or citizen, out-

MING TOMBS

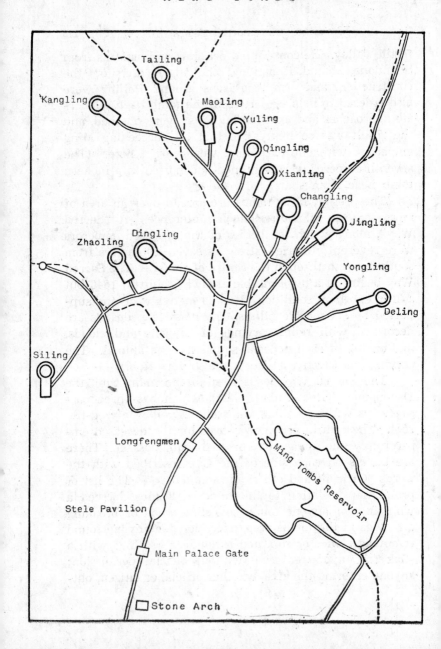

sider or guard, had to dismount a hundred paces before the gate on pain of punishment for disrespect. The wall surrounding the tombs was 40 kilometres long. Along it were ten passes, each with a fortress building guarded by imperial troops. Most of the wall and buildings had collapsed before Liberation but remains can still be seen here and there.

At some distance inside the gate is the stele pavilion, with a white stone *huabiao* at each of its four corners. Inside the pavilion is a tall stele about 6.5 metres high. The stele rests on the back of a stone tortoise and has a dragon's head on its top. The front of the tablet bears an inscription in the hand of the fourth Ming emperor, Hongxi: "Tablet of the Divine Merit and Sagely Virtue of Changling[name of Yongle's tomb] of the Great Ming"; on the reverse is an inscription by Qianlong.

Beyond the stele pavilion is an impressive array of 24 stone animals followed by twelve stone human figures along both sides of the Sacred Way. The procession starts with four lions, four *xiezhai* (mythical beasts), four camels, four elephants, four *qilin* (mythical beasts) and four horses. In each group one pair is standing and the other kneeling down. The human figures are four military officials, four civil officials and four meritorious officials. The statues are each carved out of a single piece of white marble, and the biggest occupies a space of up to 30 cubic metres including pedestal. The practice of placing stone animals before imperial tombs, symbolizing royal power and privilege, can be traced back as far as the Qin and Han dynasties, some two thousand years ago.

At the end of the sculpture avenue is the Longfengmen (Dragon and Phoenix Gate), also known as the Lingxingmen (Lattice Gate), consisting of three parallel small archways. Beyond the gate are the paths to the separate tombs, each ending with a Minglou (Visible Tower), the tallest building in the area. Further on are the tumuli, and beneath them are the stone "underground palaces" where the emperors' coffins lie.

Construction work on the buildings along the Sacred Way lasted through several reigns until the middle of the 16th century. The Sacred Way was originally built for the Changling (Yongle's tomb), but as the rest of the tombs were built to the right and left it became the main approach to all of them. Although they form one group, each tomb is independent from the rest. Each lies at the foot of a hill, and the distance between two tombs ranges from 0.25 kilometre to four kilometres. Apart from the Siling in the southwest, they are clustered in one area around the Changling.

The tombs built by the emperors for themselves are all on a grand scale, for example, the Changling, the Yongling and the Dingling; those built by the deceased emperors' successors were generally small, such as the Xianling and the Jingling. The largest and most interesting are the Changling and the Dingling, which are also the only two open to the public.

The Changling

The Changling contains the remains of Yongle, the third Ming emperor whose reign lasted from 1403 to 1424, and those of his empress who died in 1407. It is the first and biggest tomb, and occupies the central position at the end of the Sacred Way. The first courtyard now contains only a stele pavilion; the storehouse and kitchen which used to stand along the east wall and west wall are no longer extant. Fruit trees and flowers now decorate the empty yard. At the rear is the Ling'enmen (Gate of Prominent Favour), leading to the more spacious second courtyard.

At the rear of the second courtyard is the imposing Ling'endian (Hall of Prominent Favour), where sacrifices were offered to the deceased emperor. The hall stands on a three-tiered marble terrace covering an area of 1,956 square metres. Nine bays wide, with a double roof of yellow glazed tiles and vermilion walls, and constructed throughout of *nanmu* (a fine hardwood), it is one of the largest wooden buildings in China. The interior is even more striking. Thirty-two huge gilded pillars of *nanmu* support the coffered ceiling, each made of a single trunk. The four largest pillars are each 1.17 metres in diameter, and were decorated with gilded lotus flower designs. The timber came from the mountains in southwest China, and took five to six years to transport to Beijing.

In the third and last courtyard is a small building known as the Minglou (Visible Tower). In the centre is a stele inscribed: "The Tomb of Emperor Chengzu of the Great Ming"; it is a replacement of the original which was destroyed by lightning. Behind the Minglou is a tumulus covered with pines and cypresses, called the Baoding (Precious Dome). Beneath the tumulus is the underground palace where the emperor is buried. The mound is 340 metres in diameter and more than one kilometre in circumference.

The cruel practice of burying the living with the dead was carried out in the first three Ming tombs, the Changling, the Xianling and the Jingling. The emperors' concubines and female attendants were first forced to commit suicide, then buried in a brick pit called "well".

The East and West Wells can still be seen in the tombs area. This practice did not end until the death of Zhu Qizhen, the sixth emperor, who left instructions for its abolition.

The Dingling

The next most famous tomb in the Ming necropolis is the Dingling, the tomb of the thirteenth emperor, Zhu Yijun, and his two empresses Xiaoduan and Xiaojing. Zhu Yijun had become emperor at the age of ten and occupied the throne for 48 years, the longest of all 16 Ming emperors, and is best known by his reign title Wanli. Wanli began to build his own tomb in 1585 as a young man of 22. It took six years to complete and cost eight million taels of silver, equalling two years' land taxes for the whole country. During the busy construction period, according to historical chronicles, over 30,000 men took part in the work every day.

The Dingling was constructed on a vast scale with magnificent building, and ranks third after the Changling and Yongling. However, nothing of the buildings are left standing today except the Minglou, the Baoding and the foundations of the Ling'endian, similar to those at the Changling. When the tomb was completed, Wanli celebrated with a banquet in his funeral chamber. Afraid of tomb robbers, he had the tomb built very solidly and arranged that after his burial it would be strictly sealed. For centuries after his death in 1620, the underground palace was locked in mystery.

In 1956, Chinese archaeologists began the excavation of the Dingling underground palace. This was the first excavation at the Ming Tombs.

The underground palace is hidden 27 metres below

the surface, and occupies a total of 1,195 square metres of floor space. It consists of five spacious halls: an antechamber, central hall, rear hall and left and right annexes. The vaulted halls are built of stone, without a single beam or column. The antechamber and central hall form a long passageway, at the end of which is the rear hall set at right angles, in the form of a T.

In front of the antechamber, central hall and rear hall are white marble doors, all similar in appearance with an arched passageway and exquisite carvings on all sides. Each panel of the doors is 3.3 metres high, 1.7 wide and weighs four tons.

The floors are paved with specially-made square-bricks called "golden bricks". Each brick was fired for over a hundred days in a kiln heated by wood from several kinds of trees, and then given a final soaking in tung oil. To make 50,000 bricks in this way took three years, but the bricks are smooth and shiny, and hard wear only makes them more polished.

The antechamber is only an entrance to the central hall or sacrificial chamber. At the rear of the hall are three white marble thrones, for the emperor and his two consorts. Before each throne is a set of five glazed pottery altar-pieces, consisting of two pricket candlesticks, two beakers and an incense burner, each piece standing on a carved white marble pedestal. These altar-pieces signify that even after death the emperor still sits on high, receiving the homage of his subjects and exercising rule over all. In front of each set is a blue-and-white porcelain tub of oil, with the "everlasting lamp", a bronze bowl with a wick, floating on its surface. The lamp was lit when the emperor was buried, but after the tomb was closed, the flame soon died for want of oxygen.

The two annexes are similar to the antechamber and central hall. Each contains a white marble dais evidently intended for a coffin.

The rear hall is 30.1 metres long, 9.1 metres wide and 9.5 metres high, and is the largest of the five chambers. In the centre is a dais on which is placed the coffin of the Wanli emperor, with the coffins containing the First Empress on his left and the Second Empress on his right. Each coffin was surrounded by pieces of jade which were thought to preserve the bodies from decay. Also on the dais were four pairs of *meiping* porcelain vases and 26 red lacquered wooden boxes filled with precious funeral objects.

The vaulted ceiling had already come into wide use in Chinese tomb construction by the Han dynasty. The most important feature is its ability to bear great pressure. The vaulted ceilings of the underground palace of the Dingling, constructed out of huge stone blocks, are even more solid than previous vaulted tombs made of bricks, so that over several centuries not a single stone has worked loose or fallen away. The transportation of the enormous quantities of stone, wood and bricks needed for such a huge tomb was a mammoth undertaking which could only be carried out in winter. The builders had to dig a well every half kilometre along specially-opened roads, and in the depths of winter pour water over the road to form an icy surface over which the stones could be dragged. According to the records, it took 28 days and altogether 20,000 men to pull a stone 10 metres long, 3.3 metres wide and 1.3 metres thick over the ice roads from Fangshan on the outskirts of Beijing where it was quarried to the construction site.

The Dingling contained a very large number of precious objects buried with the emperor. Many of them have been excavated, including gold plates, basins, cups, bowls and spoons of various sizes, gold and silver ingots, and jewels. Most of the gold and silver objects are exquisitely engraved, some inlaid with rubies and emeralds. Many are marked with the date of manufacture, the name of the object and its weight; some also have the names of the makers and the supervising officials. The most valuable of the tomb's treasures are a gold crown and four phoenix crowns. The gold crown was the emperor's imperial crown. It is made of very fine gold thread woven into a filagree bonnet and decorated at the back with two dragons sporting with a pearl. It is the first imperial crown uncovered in excavations in China.

The phoenix crowns were worn by the empresses at grand ceremonies. Four of them have been excavated. They are decorated with various combinations of dragons and phoenixes, such as twelve dragons and nine phoenixes on one crown, or six dragons and three phoenixes on another. The dragons are made of gold and carry pearls in their mouths. Each crown was inlaid with 5,000 pearls of different sizes and a hundred precious stones, each costing 500 to 600 taels of silver. These stones are said to have been bought from Sri Lanka and India.

Besides gold and silver articles, large amounts of porcelain, jade and cloth were found in the tomb. The porcelain includes blue-and-white ware, a famous product of the Ming dynasty which was sold to Africa, Europe and other parts of Asia at the beginning of the 15th century. More than 300 pieces of cloth were found, mainly robes and rolls of silk. The cloth is woven in beautiful patterns, and the majority are interwoven with gold

The Thirteen Imperial Tombs of the Ming Dynasty

Tomb	Emperor	Reign title	Reign period
Changling	Zhu Di	Yongle	1403 - 1424
Xianling	Zhu Gaochi	Hongxi	1425
Jingling	Zhu Zhanji	Xuande	1426 - 1435
Yuling	Zhu Qizhen	Zhengtong	1436 - 1449
		Tianshun	1457 - 1464
Maoling	Zhu Jianshen	Chenghua	1465 - 1487
Tailing	Zhu Youcheng	Hongzhi	1488 - 1505
Kangling	Zhu Houzhao	Zhengde	1506 - 1621
Yongling	Zhu Houzong	Jiajing	1522 - 1566
Zhaoling	Zhu Zaihou	Longqing	1567 - 1572
Dingling	Zhu Yijun	Wanli	1573 - 1620
Qingling	Zhu Changluo	Taichang	1620
Deling	Zhu Youxiao	Tianqi	1621 - 1627
Siling	Zhu Youjian	Chongzhen	1628 - 1644

Note: Zhu Qiyu, who reigned between 1450 and 1456 when his brother Zhu Qizhen was a prisoner of war, was deposed and later buried at Jin Hill on the western outskirts of Beijing. The other 13 emperors from Zhu Di to Zhu Youjian were all entombed at the foot of Tianshou Hill.

thread, some of which remains bright and glittering even today. The emperor's dragon robe was embroidered with 12 dragons, all in different shapes. The long gown of the childless Empress Xiaoduan was embroidered with figures of a hundred young boys, and the Chinese character for longevity with two dragons, as well as pines, bamboos, plums, pomegranates and palm trees embroidered in gold thread.

The Qing Tombs

The imperial tombs of the Qing dynasty lie in three sites. The early Qing rulers, whose rule did not extend beyond north China, were buried in Shenyang, hundred of kilometres northeast of Beijing. The Qing emperors who ruled over the whole country were buried in Hebei near Beijing. The two sites in Hebei, known as the Eastern and Western Qing Tombs, are very beautiful but attract fewer visitors than the Ming Tombs because of their greater distance from the capital.

The Eastern Tombs (Dongling)

This is the largest and most complete group of imperial tombs in China. Located in Malanyu in Zunhua County,[1] Hebei, about 125 kilometres east of Beijing, it contains fifteen tombs for five Qing emperors and their empresses, concubines and daughters, including the notorious Empress Dowager Cixi. The tombs for the emperors and empresses are roofed with yellow glazed tiles, but concubines were only entitled to green glazed tiles. Altogether 157 people were buried here, in a site that covers 48 square kilometres.

[1]遵化。

The tombs lie at the foot of the Changrui Mountains, which form a natural barrier to the north. It is said that the first Qing emperor, Shunzhi, chose the site on a hunting trip. Construction of Shunzhi's tomb began in 1663, two years after his death, using the Ming Tombs as a model. A huge archway stands before the main gate, Dahongmen (Great Red Gate), leading into the area which was originally enclosed by a wall. A Sacred Way, paved with bricks and twelve metres wide, leads from the archway to the Xiaoling, Shunzhi's tomb, directly north. Inside the main gate is the Greater Stele Pavilion, with a stele inscribed with an account in Manchu and Chinese of the accomplishments of the deceased Shunzhi. Four *huabiao* stand around the pavilion. The Sacred Way then bends slightly to the left (this was believed to avert evil) and beyond begins the avenue of stone animals and human figures, in the same arrangement as in the Ming Tombs Behind is the Longfengmen (Dragon and Phoenix Gate) and a bridge over a moat. Just before and after this point other sacred ways branch off to the right and left, leading to the other tombs. The tombs differ in size and elaborateness, but each of the imperial tombs has a Lesser Stele Pavilion, with the temple name and dynastic title of the deceased emperor inscribed in Manchu, Chinese and Mongolian; a Long'endian (Hall of Eminent Favour) containing the deceased's spirit tablet; a Minglou (Visible Tower); and a Baoding (Precious Dome), the tumulus under which the coffin rests in an underground palace. The Minglou are the highest buildings in the area. Inside each is a stele smeared with cinnabar, on which are inscribed in Manchu, Chinese and Mongolian the names of the emperors, empresses or concubines buried there.

EASTERN QING TOMBS

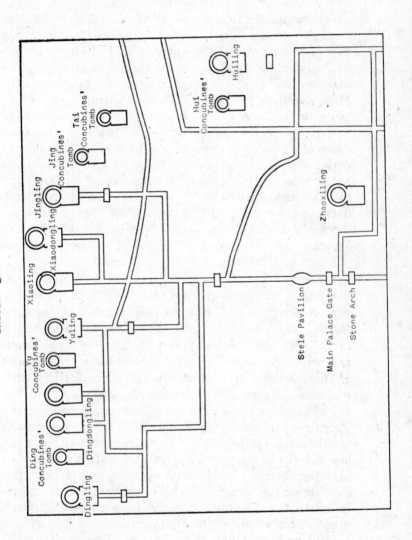

Immediately to the west of the Xiaoling is the Yuling, the tomb of the Qianlong emperor. Qianlong was the longest reigning Qing emperor and his tomb is particularly splendid, with its own avenue of animals. The underground palace has an unusual layout: unlike the Ming tombs, it is composed of three chambers with four doors, in the shape of the character *zhu* 主, meaning "ruler". It is 54 metres long and covers a total floor space of 327 square metres. Yuling was the second imperial tomb to be excavated in China and is now open to the public. It is particularly famous for its fine marble carvings, which cover the walls and ceilings with dazzling splendour. Among the most notable features are the eight bodhisattvas, four devaraja, a host of small Buddhas and thousands of Buddhist sutras carved in Sanskrit and Tibetan.

The tomb of the Empress Dowager Cixi, the Dongdingling, is further west. In terms of technical and artistic skill, its construction is the most advanced of all the Qing tombs. The marble balustrade around the main hall is carved with dragons and phoenixes sporting amid clouds and waves. The carving on the central ramp on the flight of stairs leading up to the main hall is particularly fine: it shows a dragon and a phoenix playing with a pearl in the clouds, but in a reversal of the usual pattern, the phoenix (symbolizing the empress) is above the dragon (symbolizing the emperor). The inner walls of the main and side halls are covered with gold leaf in a design of bats (symbolizing good fortune) offering the character *shou* (meaning "longevity"). The columns are completely covered with gilded dragons in semi-relief, though dragon decorations are rarely found in the tombs of empresses or concubines. The Empress Dowager's underground palace is the first such burial site of an empress to be excavated and is now open to the public. It is constructed throughout of finely carved marble.

The Eastern Qing Tombs were severely plundered and damaged by the warlord Sun Tianying in 1928, but since 1949 they have been extensively renovated. An office for the protection of the necropolis was set up in 1952 and in 1961 the site was designated a major national treasure under state protection.

The Western Tombs (Xiling)

The Western Qing Tombs are situated in Lianggezhuang in Yixian[1] County, Hebei, over 100 kilometres southwest of Beijing. The site contains four emperors' tombs, three empresses' tombs and four concubines' tombs, as well as the tombs of princes and princesses. The tombs are widely-spaced, covering a total area of over a hundred square kilometres. The Western Qing Tombs are in the same style as the Eastern Qing Tombs and are in a good state of preservation.

The first tomb to be built here was the Tailing for the third Qing emperor, Yongzheng. It is said that in the seventh year of his reign, the emperor picked this site for his tomb because he felt uneasy at the thought of lying in the same necropolis as his father. It is popularly believed that his father, the Kangxi emperor, had willed his throne to his fourteenth son and Yongzheng had altered the will to read that the successor should be the fourth son, himself. Later emperors had the choice of both sites for their burial. Construction on the Tailing began in 1730. It is the largest of the Western Tombs and

[1]易县。

WESTERN QING TOMBS

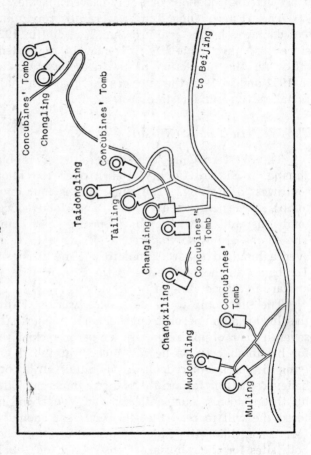

occupies the central position. A broad Sacred Way lined by pines and cypresses marks its approach.

Some of the most beautiful carvings at the Western Qing Tombs are in the main hall of the Muling tomb, where the Daoguang emperor was buried. The hall is constructed entirely of unpainted *nanmu,* whose aroma fills the room. The coffered ceiling is carved with innumerable dragons belching mouthfuls of clouds and mist. It is said that Daoguang's tomb originally was built at the Eastern Tombs site. Upon its completion, however, the emperor on his tour of inspection found that the soles of his shoes were getting damp. He suspected that this was caused by "dragons digging into the earth and spouting water from their mouths". Thereupon he ordered the tomb dismantled and had another one built at the western site. Daoguang believed that if the dragons were coaxed up to the ceiling, the underground palace would be free from waterlogging, and ordered that dragons be carved on the ceiling in a pattern of "ten thousand dragons gathering and spouting fragrance from their mouths". Therefore the dragons here are depicted issuing fragrant mists and clouds instead of water, and the underground palace is quite dry.

Since Liberation, the Western Tombs have been under government protection. Acres of pines, cypresses and other trees have been planted and now provide shade. In spring, peaches and plums blossom around the golden and vermilion halls, and in autumn, apples and persimmons add their colour to the scenery.

The Eastern and Western
Imperial Tombs of the Qing Dynasty

Tomb	Emperor	Reign title	Reign period
Eastern Tombs			
Xiaoling	Aisin-Gioro Fulin	Shunzhi	1644 – 1661
Jingling	Aisin-Gioro Xuanye	Kangxi	1662 – 1722
Yuling	Aisin-Gioro Hongli	Qianlong	1736 – 1795
Dingling	Aisin-Gioro Yizhu	Xianfeng	1851 – 1861
Huiling	Aisin-Gioro Zaichun	Tongzhi	1862 – 1874
Western Tombs			
Tailing	Aisin-Gioro Yinzhen	Yongzheng	1723 – 1735
Changling	Aisin-Gioro Yongyan	Jiaqing	1796 – 1820
Muling	Aisin-Gioro Minning	Daoguang	1821 – 1850
Chongling	Aisin-Gioro Zaitian	Guangxu	1875 – 1908

7

Temples, Mosques and Churches

Since the 13th century when it became the capital of a unified China, Beijing has been the centre of Chinese religious activities. The temples, mosques and churches around the city are not only places for religious worship but also repositories for historical and artistic treasures.

Buddhist Temples

Most of the temples in Beijing today are Buddhist. Buddhism originated in India around the 6th or 5th century B.C., based on the teachings of the historical figure, Gautama or Prince Siddhartha, also known as Sakyamuni (the wise one of the Sakya tribe). A later form of Buddhism, known as Mahayana (Great Vehicle), reached China in the first century A.D. and flourished particularly in the centuries up to the Tang dynasty. Many different sects developed in China, the most famous being the *Chan* (Japanese: *Zen*) sect which has some similarities to Taoism.

Chinese Buddhism has a substantial pantheon based on several tiers of divine beings. At the highest level are the Buddhas, who have achieved perfection and dwell in Nirvana. Chief among them is Sakyamuni, who is usually depicted sitting in meditation or sometimes in a recumbent position signifying his entrance into Nirvana. He is often shown as the central figure in one of several trinities. One is the trinity of the three ages: the Buddha of the Present is Sakyamuni; the Buddha of the Past is Kasyapa (Chinese: *Jiayefo*); and the Buddha of the Future is Maitreya (*Milofo*). Another trinity often found in *Chan* temples is formed with Sakyamuni, Amitabha (*Emitofo*) and Bhaisajyaguru (*Yaoshifo*, the god of medicine). A third trinity has Sakyamuni flanked by Vairochana (*Piluzhena*) representing the law (*fa*) or doctrine and Lochana (*Lushena*) representing the priesthood (*seng*).

On the second level are the bodhisattvas, beings who have achieved perfection but who remain in this world to relieve suffering and lead others to salvation. Maitreya, the Bodhisattva of the Future, is a particularly popular figure in this world. Known to the West as the "Laughing Buddha", he is usually depicted smiling broadly and with his ample chest and belly exposed. Another extremely popular bodhisattva is Avalokitesvara, known to the Chinese as Guanyin, the Goddess of Mercy. It is probable that Guanyin is a native Chinese deity for whom an Indian counterpart was later found. Three other bodhisattvas commonly found depicted in Chinese temples are Manjusri (*Wenshu*), the Bodhisattva of Wisdom, who rides a lion; Samantabhadra (*Puxian*), the Bodhisattva of Universal Kindness, who rides a white elephant; and Ksitigarbha (*Dizang*), the Bodhisattva of the Earth.

The third group are the arhats (*luohan*), who have been commanded to stay in this world and preach the doctrines of the Buddha. They are usually shown in a group of ten (the first ten disciples of Buddha) or of eighteen (including the famous Chinese monk Xuanzang, 596-664). Two of the first group, Ananda (*Onan*) and Kasyapa (*Jiaye*; not the same as the Buddha Kasyapa), are often depicted standing directly before the Buddha.

Apart from these three groups there are also various tutelary gods, guardian spirits and the patriarchs of different Buddhist sects.

Chinese Buddhist temples usually consist of a group of central halls arranged on a south-north axis, separated into courtyards and with lesser buildings to the east and west. Entering the forecourt through the main gate, and passing by the drum and bell towers to either side the visitor is usually welcomed by a smiling Maitreya in a small hall or chapel, over whom the four devaraja (*tian-wang*: heavenly kings) stand guard. Behind the altar and facing the inner temples is Veda (*Weito*), the head of the heavenly guards, who is usually depicted as very fierce and who holds a *vajra* (mace); in this position he can guard the inner sanctuary without frightening away visitors. The main hall or sanctuary, in the second court-yard, often houses one of the Buddha trinities. Other halls behind may be dedicated to the patron Buddha, bodhisattva or patriarch of the temple. A two-storeyed library for the Tripitaka often stands at the rear. The courtyards are often paved and set with fine old trees, shrubs and ponds; steles, *ding* (tripods) and other antique and beautiful objects also decorate the temples and courtyards. Behind the main temples are the residences of the abbots, meditation rooms, and the rear, often a big pagoda (*ta* or *baota*).

The Guangjisi (Temple of Vast Succour)

Situated east of the Xisi crossroads, this temple was first built in the Jin (Jurchen) dynasty and renovated in the Chenghua reign of the Ming dynasty and renamed Hongci Guangjisi (Temple of Wide Mercy and Vast Succour). In its long history it has seen many periods of prosperity and decline. The present buildings were constructed in 1935 after a fire. After Liberation the temple was repaired with the help of the people's government and now serves as the headquarters of the Buddhist Association of China.

The temple is arranged around four courtyards. In the forecourt are a bell tower and a drum tower, now no longer in use. Behind them is the Miledian (Maitreya Hall), built in 1952; it contains images of Maitreya and Veda, but the four devaraja are missing. In the second courtyard stand five steles, three from the Ming dynasty and two from the Qing. The inscriptions on the Ming steles have been obliterated, but the inscriptions by the Kangxi and Qianlong emperors on the other two provide valuable information about the temple's history. There is also a fine bronze *ding* on a marble base dated 1793. To the east and west are the offices and library of the Buddhist Association.

The main sanctuary is the Daxiongdian (Mahavira Hall), which houses wooden images of the Buddhas of the Three Ages (Sakyamuni, Kasyapa and Maitreya) dating from the Ming dynasty. At the sides of the hall are bronze statues of the 18 arhats, also dating from the Ming. Behind the altar, facing north, is a "finger painting" by the Qing artist Fu Wen.[1] Measuring five by ten metres, it is the largest such painting in China, and was

[1]傅雯。

completed in 1745. It depicts more than a hundred people listening to Sakyamuni preaching at Gridhrakuta. To
his right and left are Manjusri riding a black lion and
Samantabhadra on a white elephant; the devaraja guard
him overhead, and Kasyapa and Ananda stand before
him.

In the third courtyard is the Yuantongdian (Hall of
Accommodating Tact), dedicated to Guanyin. The statue
of Guanyin with a thousand eyes and a thousand arms
which used to stand at the central altar has been removed to the Fayuansi. The long altar now contains a gilded
wooden statue of Guanyin dating from the Ming, a
bronze Guanyin riding an animal, and a lacquer-work
Tala Guanyin (Tibetan) seated on a lotus. A small modern Guanyin stands on a table near the entrance. The
walls previously had murals but are now blank.

The fourth and last courtyard contains the two-
storeyed Shelige (Sarira Pavilion) for housing Buddhist
relics. The valuable library of rare books and art objects formerly housed in the east wing and upper storey
of this building have now been removed to the Fayuansi.
The ground floor, now called Duobaodian (Hall of Many
Treasures), contains an exhibition of gifts donated by
foreign countries and Buddhist associations abroad. In
the centre is a stone replica of a Sakyamuni image from
Sri Lanka personally brought to China by the Prime Minister of Sri Lanka in 1979.

The Guangjisi is a major centre for Buddhist activities in Beijing. On the 1st, 8th, 15th and 23rd of each
lunar month Buddhists come here to worship. A small
community of monks lives here and tends the grounds.
The main functions of the Buddhist Association are worship, research and publishing, and maintaining contacts

with Buddhists abroad. Since the temple reopened in 1973, it has received visits from overseas Buddhists wishing to learn about China's policy on Buddhism and to carry out scholarly exchanges; the number has increased greatly since 1977.

The Fayuansi (Temple of the Source of the Law)

This famous Buddhist temple lies at the southern end of Xizhuan Hutong, beyond Xuanwumen (Gate of Military Virtue). Emperor Taizong (Li Shimin) of the Tang dynasty decided to build a temple here in 645 in memory of his generals and soldiers who had fallen in battle. Construction was carried out in 696 under Empress Wu Zetian, and the temple was named the Minzhongsi (Temple to Mourn the Loyal). Most of the temple buildings were destroyed by the Liao although the temple was to the southeast of the Tang city. In the Jin (Jurchen) dynasty examinations for the selection of officials were held here. The temple was destroyed by wars and earthquakes (the one which caused most serious damage was in 1075) and restored again several times during its long history. Its present layout was determined during the Ming dynasty, and most of the present buildings and the present name date from the restoration carried out in 1734 during the Yongzheng reign of early Qing.

With an area of 6,400 square metres, the Fayuansi is second only to the Yonghegong (see below) in size. The splendid buildings and courtyards planted with lilacs, grass and many different kinds of trees create an atmosphere of beauty and tranquility.

The Fayuansi has been for many years the repository of valuable Buddhist objects and historical treasures.

During the "cultural revolution", however, the buildings and their treasures were seriously damaged or destroyed. Extensive restoration was carried out in 1977, and many newly excavated objects or objects from other temples were brought here. Legacies from the Ming include the gilded bronze statues of Veda (Skanda) and the devaraja in the Devaraja Hall and the 18 arhats in the Mahavira Hall in the first and second courtyards. The pillar foundations in the Mahavira Hall date from the Tang. In the third courtyard is the Terrace of Mourning for the Loyal with three tablets (one broken) from the Tang and three incomplete *zhuang* (pillars) dating from the Liao. Despite the erosion of several centuries the inscriptions can still be deciphered, making them important material for research on the temple's history and the political and social life of the time. Behind is the Pilufodian (Vairochana Hall), formerly memorial hall for the famous Tang dynasty monk Xuanzang. It contains a five-in-one bronze image of Vairochana seated on a lotus throne and facing south, north, east, west and the centre, also dating from the Ming. The base of the throne is carved with a thousand Buddhas and the lotus is supported by four Buddhas. The exquisite workmanship demonstrates the advanced level of metallurgical techniques in Ming China. A museum in the fifth courtyard contains valuable manuscripts, ceramics, bronzes and other treasures.

Since Liberation the Fayuansi has been an important centre for Buddhist activities. The Buddhist Academy was founded here in 1956, and reopened in 1978. The Chinese Buddhist Association carries out scholarly research here and receives Buddhists from other parts of China and abroad. The temple's meditation halls are open to Chinese and foreign Buddhists for worship, offering incense, meditating and chanting sutras. In October 1956, an international delegation of Buddhist monks from Thailand, Burma, Nepal, Cambodia and Sri Lanka made a visit here, and in 1963 it was the site of the Congress of Asian Buddhists. In May 1980, a Japanese delegation brought over a statue of the famous Tang dynasty monk Jianzhen[1] to be exhibited here. More than 1,200 years ago, Jianzhen made the difficult passage to Japan, bringing Chinese Buddhism and Chinese culture, arts, architecture and medicine to the Japanese, contributing to cultural interchange between the two countries.

The Biyunsi (Temple of Azure Clouds)

Lying on the east slope of the Western Hills, its east-west axis following the contours of the terrain, this temple is the most splendid and beautiful in the area. Construction began on a convent here called the Biyun'an (Convent of Azure Clouds) in the Yuan dynasty, and the buildings were enlarged in the 16th century. In the Qing dynasty, it became a popular spot for excursions by the emperors and their concubines. In 1748, during the Qianlong reign, further extensions were made: the Hall of the Five Hundred Arhats was built after the Jingcisi (Temple of Pure Benevolence) in Hangzhou and the Diamond Throne Pagoda was erected on the hill behind the temple.

The temple is constructed on six different levels from the entrance gate to the pagoda at the summit, due to the steepness of the site, and has a series of interconnecting courtyards, each with its own special character.

[1] 鉴真。

Before the entrance gate lies a white stone bridge over a deep gully, along which flows a clear stream. Locust trees, willows, pines and cypresses provide shelter from the sun, and a pair of fierce-looking skilfully-carved stone lions guard the bridge. Beyond the gate is the first courtyard, with a devaraja hall, drum and bell towers to either side, and a Maitreya Hall at the rear. In the second courtyard is a hall dating from the Ming with a statue of Buddha. On the next level is the Hall of the Five Bodhisattvas and behind it is the Sun Yat-sen Memorial Hall.

The Hall of the Five Hundred Arhats is in a side courtyard to the south. As is usual in these halls, each arhat is portrayed in a different pose and with a different expression. The sculpture is finely executed in a very realistic style. Each figure is about 1.5 metres tall and they are arranged several rows deep through the building which is in the shape of a Greek cross. Apart from the arhats, there are seven other deities standing in the passageway and the minute figure of the monk Tao Ji, popularly known as Ji Gong, squatting on a roof beam. According to tradition, the monk came late and because of his junior rank could not find a seat and had to perch up in the roof.

At the highest level of the temple is the courtyard with the Diamond Throne Pagoda. This magnificent structure rises in a grove of ancient trees. It represents the pagoda in Bodh-Gaya in Bihar, India, erected in commemoration of Sakyamuni's enlightenment and attainment of Buddhahood under the pipal tree in the village. Pagodas in this style are always called Diamond Throne Pagodas after the original. The Biyunsi pagoda is 34.7 metres high and is constructed out of white mar-

ble. Its square base is several storeys high, and an inside staircase leads up to a broad open terrace. In the
middle of the terrace is a high square tower surrounded
by four smaller square pagodas and two round pagodas.
There is also a pavilion over the stairwell and a small
oratory to one side. The terrace affords a magnificent
view of Beijing and the Western Hills. The whole building is covered with exquisite relief carvings of Buddhas,
devaraja and warriors, dragons and phoenixes, lions and
elephants and cloud patterns, all in Tibetan style. Although built to a typical Indian design, the construction
and carving have also been influenced by native Chinese
styles and the result represents the high level of architectural skill reached during the Qianlong period.

After Sun Yat-sen died in Beijing in 1925 his coffin
was placed in the pagoda before being removed to Nanjing in 1929. His clothes and hat are still sealed in the
pagoda. In 1955, the hall in front of the pagoda was
converted into a Memorial Hall; side galleries contain
photographs illustrating Sun Yat-sen's life and work.

A short walk southeast of the Biyunsi is the northern
entrance of Xiangshan Park (Fragrance Hill Park); to the
west lies another famous temple, the Wofosi (Temple of
the Recumbent Buddha).

The Wofosi (Temple of the Recumbent Buddha)

The Wofosi is situated in the northwestern outskirts
of Beijing, on the slopes of the Western Hills. The temple
on this site was first built in the 7th century in the Tang
dynasty, and it is believed that at that time it already
had a statue of a recumbent Buddha. The temple was
renovated and expanded in the Yuan dynasty when it
was claimed that "fifty tons of copper" were used to

cast an enormous statue of a recumbent Buddha in 1321.
In the Ming dynasty it was restored again and renamed
the Yong'ansi (Temple of Eternal Peace), and in the Qing
dynasty it was also restored and renamed the Shifang
Pujuesi (Temple of Universal Awakening), the name it
retains to the present day. It is generally referred to as
the Wofosi, and since its restoration in 1955 it has become
a popular tourist spot.

The present Recumbent Buddha, in the fourth courtyard of the temple, may be a copy of the Yuan Buddha
or one of the other recumbent Buddhas known to have
been in the temple. It weighs about 54 tons and is 5.2
metres in length. The Buddha lies on his side, his legs
stretched out, his left arm resting on his left thigh and
his right arm bent to support his head. The figure is
well-proportioned and the pose is easy and relaxed.
Behind it is a row of the twelve disciples modelled in
clay. According to tradition, the tableau represents an
episode from the *Digha-Nikaya*, which relates how Sakyamuni issued instructions to his disciples under the
shade of a sal-tree outside Kusinagara in India, as he
neared the end of his earthly existence. At the east and
west walls are cases of embroidered cloth shoes offered
by the Qing emperors to the bare-footed Buddha.

Apart from the Recumbent Buddha, the temple is
also famous for its rare and beautiful trees. An avenue
of ancient cypresses leads up to the entrance of the temple, which is formed by a resplendent glazed-tile archway.
In the first courtyard an arched bridge spans a pool in
front of the Shanmendian (Mountain Gate Hall). In the
second courtyard are two ancient sal-trees, which are
believed to have been brought here from India when the
temple was being constructed to give an authentic set-

ting for Sakyamuni's entry into Nirvana. When they
come into blossom in early summer their pure white
flowers resemble small jade pagodas hanging down from
the dark-green leaves. Among the other trees and shrubs
are magnificent old cypresses, pines, gingkoes, locusts,
wistaria, lilac and forsythia. Even in mid-summer the
spacious grounds and shade from the trees make the
temple a cool and attractive spot.

The Front Gate, Devaraja Hall and Hall of the Buddhas of the Three Ages are open and in good condition,
but are now empty of statues and paintings. In front of
the Recumbent Buddha Hall are two steles and a bronze
ding dating from the Qianlong reign. Behind this hall is
the two-storeyed hall for Buddhist scriptures, and behind
that is the Shouanshan (Hill of Longevity and Peace), on
top of which stands a small pavilion overlooking the whole
temple. West of the main buildings are a series of three
pavilions, formerly for the use of the emperor; there is
also a rockery, a small pond spanned by a bridge, and a
beautiful large square pond covered with lotus. The last
of the pavilions is now a brightly-painted teahouse overlooking the square pond.

About half a kilometre northwest of the temple is the
Yingtaogou Huayuan (Cherry Valley Garden), an attractive small park winding up a hill in a natural woodland
setting, with a hermit's cave and a small clear stream.

The Dazhongsi (Great Bell Temple)

The Dazhongsi is situated in Haidian in the northwestern suburbs. Built in 1733 in the reign of the
Yongzheng emperor of the Qing dynasty, its formal name
is Jueshengsi (Temple of Awakening). Since the famous
great bell it houses was brought here in 1743, it has pop-

ularly been known as the Dazhongsi. The bell is known
as the Great Bell or the King of Bells: it is the largest bell
in China, and the second largest in the world. Originally
it was one of six to be hung at the six corners of the city
walls to strike the hours, but it is the only one remaining.
It is also known as the Avatamsaka Bell because it bears
the full text of all 81 volumes on the *Avatamsaka Sutra*
(*Huayanjing* or Lotus Scripture). Since the Yongle emperor ordered it cast in 1406 in the Ming dynasty, it is
also sometimes referred to as the Yongle Bell. Yongle
came to power at the turn of the 14th century after a
coup d'etat. One story says that he tried to atone for his
guilt by having the great bell cast with 17 sutras inscribed
on it. He hoped to "divert public indignation by striking
the bell", according to an "Ode to the Great Bell" inscribed on a tablet during the Daoguang reign of the Qing
dynasty. The tablet stands to one side of the bell in the
temple. The other story says that the bell was cast in
memory of the officers and men who died in the northern
campaigns.

Together with its handle, the great bell stands 6.75
metres high and weighs 46.5 tons. The outer rim of the
lip measures 3.3 metres in diameter and the inner rim
measures 2.9 metres; the thickness of the lip or sound
bow, upon which the strike or fundamental tone of the
bell depends, averages 220 mm. The sound bow is engraved with the *Vagrakkhedika Pragnaparamita* (Diamond Sutra) and the inside of the bell is engraved with
the *Avatamsaka Sutra* and the *Suvararna Prabhasa Ut-
tamaraja Sutra*. The outside is engraved with names of
Buddhas and bodhisattvas. There is altogether a total of
227,000 characters, in a boldly executed regular script

believed to be the handwriting of Shen Du,[1] a calligrapher of the Ming dynasty. The whole text can be read with ease by someone standing under the bell and looking up. Despite its 500 years, the bell shows no sign of any damage or rust. It is evidence of the high level of metallurgy during the Ming and also a valuable source for the study of metallurgy and Buddhist scriptures.

The removal of the bell from its former home in the Wanshousi (Temple of Longevity), better known as the Jietaisi (see below), to the Jueshengsi was a complex operation. First, in the depths of winter, water was poured along the roadway to form a "ice route" along which the bell was hauled to its destination by oxen. Next, at the base of the bell tower, a mound was constructed and coated with ice, and the bell was pushed up the side of the mound to come to rest on its top. A frame consisting of a rough wooden beam and four supports was constructed around it, and after the bell was suspended from the frame the mound underneath was dug away. For over two hundred years the bell was hung from this frame and even the Tangshan earthquake of 1976 failed to disturb it.

The great bell is not only famous for its size but also for its pure, deep and melodious tone. Its frequency ranges from 22 to 800 hertz. Its clear sound reaches up to 120 decibels and can be heard 50 kilometres away at night when everything is quiet, according to tests by a team of specialists from the Acoustical Research Institute of the Chinese Academy of Sciences in October 1980. Their investigations confirmed the descriptions of the bell's tone and carrying power in old records. A museum alongside the temple illustrates the history and construc-

[1]沈度。

tion of the bell, and in the forecourt is a fascinating collection of old bells arranged in chronological order, the earliest dating from the Song dynasty.

The Lingguangsi (Temple of Divine Light)

The Lingguangsi is situated on the slopes of Cuiwei-shan (Watchet Hill), south of Xiangshan. It is one of the eight old temples and monasteries scattered around the Badachu Gongyuan (Park of Eight Great Sites). During the anti-Japanese War and the War of Liberation, this rugged area was a base for the Eighth Route Army and the People's Liberation Army.

The first temple on this site was the Longquansi (Dragon Spring Temple), which dates back to the Tang dynasty in the eighth century. It was rebuilt and renamed the Jueshansi (Temple of Awakening Mountain) in 1162, in the Jin (Jurchen) dynasty, and again in the 15th century under the Ming, when it took its present name. During the eight powers' invasion of 1900, the buildings and sculptures were destroyed. Only the base of a pagoda dating back to the Liao dynasty was left. When the site was cleared, a stone casket containing a sandalwood box was found in the pagoda base. The box contained a "tooth of Buddha" and bore the words "The holy tooth of Sakyamuni", the date "23rd day of the fourth month of the seventh year Tianhui" (963 A.D.), and a prayer in Sanskrit. According to Zhao Puchu,[1] the President of the Chinese Buddhist Association, the Buddhist classics record that after Sakyamuni was cremated, four of his teeth remained. One was brought to China and was placed in the Zhaoxianta (Pagoda for Inviting Immortals) in

[1]赵朴初。

the Western Hills around Beijing in the 11th century.
In the spring of 1955 the Chinese Buddhist Association
removed the tooth to its headquarters in the Guangjisi,
and kept it in the Sarira Pavilion. In the same year a
Buddhist delegation from Burma came to Beijing in
September to take the tooth to Burma to be worshipped,
and the tooth was returned to China eight months
later. A special pagoda for the tooth's permanent
safe-keeping was built in 1959 in the north courtyard of the Lingguangsi. The new pagoda is over fifty
metres high. Its base is made of white marble and has
a lotus pedestal and a carved white marble balustrade.
The mid-section of the pagoda is decorated with relief
carvings in stone of gates, pillars and windows. The
upper section is an octagonal thirteen-storey tower made
of orange-red bricks. The closely set eaves are covered
with turquoise glazed tiles. On the top is a gilded spire.

In the south courtyard, near the base of the Liao
pagoda, is a crystal-clear pool stocked with many kinds
of goldfish. It is said that goldfish-breeding here dates
back to 1851, under the Qing. Some fish are said to be
over a hundred years old, and the biggest is over half a
metre. The pond is covered with lotus and a pavilion
stands in the centre. Behind the pool is the Taoguang'an
(Convent of Hidden Brilliance) and further north is a
Guanyin Grotto and a stone well. Nearby is the tomb of
Princess Cuiwei of the Yuan dynasty.

The Tanzhesi (Pool and Zhe Tree Temple)

In Beijing there is a common saying that "First there
was the Tanzhesi, then came Beijing", which indicates
the great age of this temple. It dates back 1,600 years to
the Jin dynasty, when it was known as Jiafusi (Temple

of Auspicious Fortune). In the Tang it was called Longquansi (Dragon Spring Temple). Because of the Dragon
Pool at its rear and the *zhe* trees (*cudrania tricuspidata*)
on the hill, it has been popularly known as the Pool and
Zhe Tree Temple, and the various formal names it has had
during its long history have been forgotten. The present
buildings mostly date from Ming or Qing.

For a long time, the Tanzhesi was one of the most
important Buddhist centres in north China. During its
heyday, it housed some 500 monks and attracted pilgrims
and visitors from other parts of China and from foreign
countries. During the "cultural revolution", however,
this temple was vandalized, with the result that most of
the buildings are empty now. So far 400,000 yuan has
been provided by the state for repair and it is estimated
that 10 times that amount will be needed to restore it
completely. Though there are no monks at present, the
Tanzhesi is one of the major attractions in Beijing and
receives many visitors every day.

The temple has a beautiful setting in the hills of
Mentougou,[1] west of Beijing. In front of the gate is a
group of ancient pines. These distinctively shaped trees
are believed to be several hundred years old. Although
the trunks are patchy, the pines are still sturdy and seem
to get stronger as they grow older.

The distribution of the main and side halls is very
regular and symmetrical, as is characteristic of Ming and
Qing temple architecture. The buildings form three main
north-south axes. Along the central axis are the Archway,
Front Gate, Devaraja Hall, Mahavira Hall and Vairochana
Pavilion. These building are of different heights but are
all spacious and imposing. To the rear of the Mahavira

[1]门头沟。

Hall is an ancient gingko tree, thirty to forty metres high: its trunk is so wide that it takes several men with arms outstretched to encircle it. It is believed to have been planted in the Liao dynasty, about a thousand years ago, but it still flourishes with many branches and dense, vivid leaves. The Qianlong emperor gave it the name "Emperor of Trees". Across to the west is another gingko, planted later. These two and many other fine old trees give the temple an air of distinction and vitality. The Vairochana Pavilion is the highest building in the temple and affords an excellent view of the temple grounds and surrounding hills.

To the east of the central axis lies a group of buildings in traditional Chinese courtyard style: the abbot's rooms and two palaces for the Qing emperors on their visits here, the Wansuigong (Emperor's Palace) and the Taihougong (Empress Dowager's Palace). With bamboo groves and a burbling stream, this courtyard is quiet and serene. Between the two halls is the Liubeiting (Floating Cups Pavilion). On the stone floor of the pavilion is a shallow channel in the shape of a coiled dragon through which the spring water is conducted. In the past, people used to float wine cups on the water so that they were carried along the channel to other spots where others would pick them up and drink the wine. This was called "floating the goblets in the winding stream" and was believed to dispel calamities.

To the west of the central axis are several courtyards including an ordination altar and a Guanyin Hall. The latter formerly contained a "prayer brick" believed to have belonged to Princess Miaoyan[1] of the Yuan, a daughter of Kublai Khan, who entered the convent here.

[1] 妙严。

She prayed on this spot every morning and evening, and as the days passed two deep footprints were formed on the brick where she stood. The historical records mention the princess becoming a nun here, but the story of the "prayer brick" is hard to verify.

Apart from the temple buildings proper, there are also the Anledian (Hall of Ease and Joy) to the front and east of the temple. The Anledian was formerly the residence of the temple's retired monks. It has now been converted into a restaurant. Further below the temple is a two-level pagoda courtyard, which contains several dozen pagodas dating from the Jin (Jurchen), Yuan, Ming and Qing dynasties. The different styles and dates of these pagodas make them valuable material in the study of pagoda architecture and history.

The Dragon Pool lies in the hills behind the temple. In the past, the water was transparently clear and spring water flowed down from the pool in a constant stream. The pool has now dried up, and of the "thousand *zhe* trees" mentioned in the old records, only a few remain to satisfy the visitor's expectations.

The Jietaisi (Ordination Terrace Temple)

This temple is situated at Ma'anshan (Saddle Hill) in the Western Hills, about ten kilometres southeast of the Tanzhesi and 35 kilometres west of the city. The history of the temple goes back 1,350 years to the initial construction of the temple in 622 under the Tang. During the Liao dynasty, a monk named Fajun founded an altar here for the ordination of novices into the Buddhist priesthood. It was repaired in the Ming dynasty and renamed Wanshousi (Longevity Temple) but is commonly known as the Jietaisi. Most of the present buildings date from the Qing.

The main sanctuary is the Mahavira Hall, and behind it is the Qianfoge (Pavilion of a Thousand Buddhas). The main hall originally contained ten carved sandalwood chairs dating from the Ming: three above, for the abbot and two elders, and three to the left and four to the right for the witnesses to the ordination ceremony. Outside the hall are two steles, one from the Jin (Jurchen) dynasty, the other from the Liao. In the northeast courtyard is the white marble Ordination Altar, consisting of three levels altogether over three metres high. The base is exquisitely carved with figures of several hundred deities. Among them are 24 figures one metre in height, wearing helmets and body armour and looking very militant, who are leading the others about one-third their size. South of the altar is the Youpolidian (Upali Hall), containing the image of the Arhat Upali, one of Buddha's ten disciples.

Just south of the altar is the pagoda courtyard, which contains two pagodas from the Liao and Yuan dynasties, still in good condition. Near the pagoda courtyard is the Mingwangdian (Hall of the Brilliant Kings) with a stone balustrade in front enclosing three *zhuang*. The six or eight sides of the *zhuang* are inscribed with Buddhist sutras and images. Two of them date from the Liao and one from the Yuan; all three are in perfect condition. Wild flowers growing within the grounds accentuate the quiet beauty of the temples. The Jietaisi is also noted for its ancient and distinctively shaped pines, including one growing out of the terrace wall. It also has a "sensitive pine": if one branch is touched the whole tree quivers.

About two and a half kilometres west of the temple rises the Jilefeng (Great Joy Peak) below which are beautiful limestone caves with many stalagmites and stalactites, and clear spring water. Visitors to the temple may pause here on the way.

The Yonghegong (Palace of Harmony and Peace) Lamasery

At the north end of Yonghegong Street in the city's East District stands a famous lamasery with red walls and yellow tiled roofs, designated in 1961 one of China's major national treasures under state protection. Extensive restoration has been undertaken since 1979.

Lamaism is a form of Buddhism which contains a large element of Hinduism and popular Tibetan religious worship. "Lama" means "superior one". According to tradition, Buddhism entered Tibet in the 8th century, where it soon became influenced by native cults. In the 13th century it spread rapidly into Mongolia and north China. Lamaism was especially encouraged by the Qianlong emperor as a means of maintaining political unity with Mongolia and Tibet.

The lamasery, built in 1694, was originally the residence of the Yongzheng emperor before he ascended the throne. Because of the rule that a former imperial residence could not revert to secular use, it was renamed the Yonghegong and declared a lama temple. When Yongzheng died in 1735 his coffin was placed here. His successor, the Qianlong emperor, upgraded the Yonghegong to the status of an imperial palace and its green tiles were replaced by yellow ones (yellow was the imperial colour of the Qing dynasty). In 1744, it was formally converted into a lamasery (lama monastery).

The Yonghegong contains five main halls along a north-south axis. A long forecourt beyond a glazed-tile arch leads to the first main courtyard, which contains two stele pavilions, the drum and bell towers and two fine bronze lions from the Qianlong period. At the rear is the Devaraja Hall, formerly the entrance to Yong-zheng's residence, it now has a statue of Maitreya flanked by the four devaraja. Behind the altar stands Veda with a *vajra* (mace) in his hand. Immediately behind the hall is a bronze *ding* (tripod), 1.4 metres high with a dark lustrous patina. Around the top are six pairs of dragons each playing with a pearl, and at its base are three lions playing with a ball, all very skilfully carved. It is said that there are only two such *ding* in China.

Beyond the *ding* is the square Yubiting (Pavilion of the Imperial Writing-Brush) with curved eaves and a double roof. It contains a stele inscribed in Han, Man-chu, Mongolian and Tibetan, explaining the significance and origin of Lamaism. Behind the pavilion is a bronze replica in miniature of Mount Sumeru, standing in the centre of a white marble pond with a stone base carved with Buddhist images. According to Buddhist tradition, Mount Sumeru (or Mount Meru) is the centre of the world, above which lies paradise. The position of the stars below the top peak roughly corresponds to the find-ings of modern astronomy. This replica was made dur-ing the Wanli reign of the Ming dynasty and was later moved to this spot.

At the rear of the courtyard is the Mahariva Hall, known as the Yonghedian (Hall of Harmony and Peace). The central altar has the Buddhas of the Three Ages: Sakyamuni, Kasyapa to the right and Maitreya to the left.

Along the east and west walls are the 18 arhats. There are also two bodhisattvas, Ksitigarbha in the northeast corner and Maitreya (in the incarnation of a bodhisattva) in the northwest corner, and four wooden prayer wheels.

Behind the Yonghedian is the Yongyoudian (Hall of Everlasting Protection). On the altar is a statue of Amitayus, with Bhaisajyaguru to the right and Simhanada (Shihoufu) to the left. On the west wall are two fine embroidered pictures of the White Para and Green Para (incarnations of Guanyin) dating from the Qianlong reign.

The next main hall is the Falundian (Hall of the Wheel of the Law), seven bays wide. On the altar is a bronze statue, 5.5 metres high, of Tsongkhapa (1357-1419), the founder of the Yellow Sect of Lamaism. Born in Qinghai, Tsongkhapa was a great religious reformer who attempted to restore monastic discipline to Lamaism; his adherents wore yellow robes to distinguish them from the older red-robed sects. Five of Tsongkhapa's incarnations are portrayed on his nimbus. At the rear of the altar is the elaborate "Mountain of Five Hundred Arhats". The mountain itself is carved out of red sandalwood, and the arhats are modelled out of five metals (gold, silver, bronze, iron and tin). Along the east and west walls are two well-preserved sets of important scriptures in Tibetan, totalling 315 works. Also on display are two scriptures printed in gold Tibetan script, *The Scripture of the Great White Canopy Rituals* and *The Scriptures of Bhaisajyaguru*. The east and west walls are covered with colourful murals depicting episodes in Sakyamuni's missionary work.

The final hall is the Wanfuge (Pavilion of Ten

Thousand Happinesses), also known as the Dafolou (Tower of the Great Buddha), the tallest building in the Yonghegong. The central tower is three storeys high and is linked to the two-storeyed pavilions on either side by flying galleries. Wooden structures of this kind are rare in China. In the middle of the temple rises the statue of Maitreya, eighteen metres above ground and eight metres below ground. The statue is carved from a single trunk of white sandalwood, eight metres in diameter, a gift sent to the Qianlong emperor by the Seventh Dalai Lama. Qianlong had felt that the area at the rear of the original palace was too bare, and planned to erect a high tower as a protective screen. His complaint that he lacked a great statue of the Buddha to put in it was conveyed back home by Tibetan envoy. The Dalai Lama therefore had this huge sandalwood trunk sent to him. The statue was carved in a mat-shed behind the Falundian.

To the east of the Wanfuge stands the Zhaofolou (Tower of the Shining Buddha), where Qianlong's mother used to pray. The "sandalwood Buddha" on the altar is actually made of bronze and not of sandalwood, and his water-patterned robe is carved in easy, flowing lines. Originally there was a five-Buddha gold crown on his head, a pearl on his forehead and a gold umbrella over him, but these were stolen on the eve of Liberation. The shrine is made of *nanmu* (a fine hardwood) and is the largest and finest wooden carving in the temple.

The side hall to the east of the Falundian is dedicated to the five great Vajra (Guardian) bodhisattvas. It also contains two large bears modelled after the two bears weighing 500 kilos and 450 kilos caught by Qianlong in 1754 on a hunting expedition in Elengjiamu in Jiling. The west hall contains a sandalwood Buddha with

Ananda and Kasyapa by his left and right sides; ranged along the side walls are eight great bodhisattvas.

East of the Yongyoudian is the Bhaisajyaguru Hall where the lamas studied medicine. The altar shows Tsongkhapa in the centre with Bhaisajyaguru, the God of Medicine, to the south and Amitayus to the north. The west side hall is the Mathematics Hall where the lamas studied astronomy with objects such as a terrestrial globe and astroscope. The altar contains an image of Tsongkhapa and two of his disciples. East of the Yubiting is the Esoteric Hall, where the lamas studied esoteric scriptures. West is the Exoteric Hall where lectures on Buddhist philosophy were given. The Bhaisajyaguru Hall, Mathematics Hall, Esoteric Hall and Exoteric Hall are known as the "Four Study Halls", and illustrate the dual functions of Buddhism in expounding Buddhist philosophy and spreading science and culture.

Islamic Mosques

Islam is the religious faith of Muslims, or Muhammadans (followers of the Prophet Muhammed). Originally an Arab religion, it was introduced into China by Arab and Persian traders in the 7th century during the Tang dynasty. Some of the traders settled in China and formed their own communities in the northwest, southwest and southeast; converts were also made among the Han Chinese. Islam today in China is mostly practised among ten of China's minority ethnic groups, especially those of Turkic origin, such as the Hui, Uygur, Kazak, Ozbek, Tajik, Tatar, Kirgiz and so on, and mosques can be found throughout the country. The Chinese Islamic Association was founded in 1953.

Mosques are known as qingzhensi (temples of purity) or libaisi (temples of worship) in Chinese. They are usually rectangular in construction, with a large open courtyard, a covered prayer hall, side rooms for ritual ablution (a necessary step before worship), and one or more minarets from which the muezzin announces the call to prayer. The building often features one or more cupolas. The orientation of the building is determined by the direction in which Mecca lies, and a niche is set into the far end of the prayer hall to mark the direction in which the worshippers must face. This niche, the mithrab, is often richly ornamented.

The Niujie Libaisi (Ox Street Mosque)

The Niujie Libaisi is situated in the Ox Street in the Xuanwu District in the southern part of Beijing. The area has long been known as a Muslim centre, and the street was apparently named for the importance of beef in the Muslim diet (Muslims do not eat pork, the staple meat of the Han). A mosque was first built at this site in 996 in the Song dynasty. Three hundred years later, with the support of the Ming government, it was enlarged and raised to the status of one of the four official temples in Beijing. The present layout dates from the Kangxi reign of the Qing dynasty when it was enlarged and restored again. Further restoration work was carried out in 1955 and 1979.

The Niujie Libaisi is the biggest in Beijing. It covers 5,800 square metres and is built in Chinese style around three courtyards. The main front gate is used only on ceremonial occasions; directly inside it is the

Wangyuelou (Tower for Observing the Moon), a hexagonal observation tower for astronomical calculations, built in traditional Chinese style. Usual entry to the mosque is through a passageway to the south of the front gate, which leads beyond the Prayer Hall past the ablution rooms and living quarters of the imam and other religious personnel. In the rear courtyard is a minaret, from which the faithful are called to worship five times a day. Entry to the Prayer Hall, which occupies the centre of the mosque, is from the rear courtyard.

The Prayer Hall consists of three sections which altogether provide room for a thousand worshippers. An extension in front dates from the Qing dynasty, and is screened from the inner hall by a latticed door. The inner hall, dating from the Ming dynasty, has five lanes running north-south for prayer mats, intersected by five east-west naves. At the rear is one lane for prayer mats and three vaulted chambers dating from the Song dynasty. The Ming section is particularly striking with its gold-inscribed Arabic-style arches along the naves, its pillars which are inscribed in gold with sayings from the Qur'an (Koran) in Arabic and a lotus and arabesque pattern, and the elaborately decorated ceiling in Chinese style. A section to the north is screened off for female worshippers. The central chamber at the rear is built of wood and has an elaborate coffered ceiling. The mithrab has a Chinese wooden upper structure on a stone base. Such a building as this with three distinct sections from different dynasties and incorporating both Chinese and Arabic styles is very rare.

The mosque also contains two Ming dynasty steles and one Qing dynasty stele, engraved in Chinese and other languages. The Ming steles are housed in Chinese-style pavilions in the rear courtyard; one is in excellent condition, and its clearly legible script records the designation of the mosque as an official temple. In the southeastern corner of the mosque is a graveyard with two Yuan tombs; the tombstones record in Arabic the names of the two imams buried in the tombs who came from Iran and Bokhara to preach the faith in China during the reign of Kublai Khan.

A short distance away from the mosque is the headquarters of the Chinese Islamic Association, in a new three-storeyed building with three green cupolas and other elements of Middle Eastern architecture.

The Dongsi Qingzhensi (Dongsi Mosque)

The Dongsi Qingzhensi is at 13 South Dongsi Street, just northeast of the centre of town. During the five hundred or so years since it was founded under the Ming, it has been restored many times. In 1952 and again in 1974, funds were provided by the government to restore the mosque as a centre for Chinese and foreign Muslims in Beijing. It is now the headquarters of the Beijing branch of the Chinese Islamic Association.

The mosque is formed around three Chinese-style courtyards, with ablution rooms, a library and a prayer hall at the rear. The Prayer Hall is the only survival from the Ming and has now been restored to its original splendour after many years of neglect. In front is a paved courtyard planted with gingkoes and flowering shrubs. At one end of the hall verandah is a bell which used to top the minaret (no longer in existence); at the other end of the verandah is a stele with an inscription from the Wanli period of the Ming dynasty. The vestibule of the hall is a wooden structure in Chinese style.

At the rear of the hall are three brick chambers with vaulted ceilings without supporting pillars in Arabic style; the floor is painted red and carpeted. The mithrab, which should be in the central chamber, is missing. The inner hall is large and grand: the pillars are gilded with a lotus and arabesque design and the beams are painted. In the centre of the hall hangs a horizontal board with sayings from the Qur'an inscribed in Arabic. The polished wooden floor is covered with rows of prayer mats, which can accommodate five hundred people on important occasions such as 'Id al-Fitr (the breaking of Ramadan) and 'Id al-Adzha (also known as Qurban or Corban). Marriage and funeral services are also held here, and Chinese and foreign Muslims in Beijing may come for daily or weekly services. There is a separate area in the main hall for women.

The library houses valuable manuscripts of the Qur'an, the Hadith, a collection of short narratives expounding the *sunna* (tradition) of the prophet, and Islamic law, transcribed by imams in different periods in Chinese history, works of Islamic philosophy, history and literature, and Islamic classics and other works published in Egypt, India, Turkey and Pakistan. Most of the manuscripts are about two or three hundred years old; one particularly valuable manuscript of the Qur'an is 680 years old.

Christian Churches

The Nantang (Southern Cathedral)

Inside Xuanwumen in the southern part of the city is the Gothic Cathedral of the Immaculate Conception with a crucifix above its front gate, the oldest Catholic church in Beijing. With the establishment of other Catholic churches in the north, east and west of the city, it is popularly known as the Xuanwumen Catholic Church, or the Southern Cathedral of Beijing.

The spread of Catholicism (known in Chinese as Tianzhujiao, the Teachings of the Ruler of Heaven) to Beijing dates back to the end of the Ming dynasty with the arrival of the Italian Jesuit, Matteo Ricci, on January 25, 1601. Ricci took a house near Xuanwumen, where he died in 1610. The German Jesuit Schall von Bell came to Beijing in 1630 and took over Ricci's house, from where he conducted his religious activities. Schall became director of the Board of Astronomy under the Qing, and in 1650, with the help of the board, he was granted permission to build a Catholic church on this site. The church buildings included a rectory, library, observatory and instrument room. Due to earthquake, fire and rebellion, the church was twice destroyed, in 1775 and again in 1900; the only survival is a stone tablet with a barely legible inscription.

The present church dates from 1904, and is a grey brick edifice. On the altar inside is a tabernacle containing the Blessed Sacrament and a Perpetual Flame. Above the altar is a painting of the Virgin Mary, and along the walls are fourteen paintings depicting the Stations of the Cross. Inside the entrance is a choir gallery, and along the wall are three confessional boxes. Seating is provided for about a thousand worshippers. Chinese and foreign Catholics attend mass here on Sundays. Marriages, baptisms and requiem masses are also conducted here, and at Easter and Christmas more than a thousand people fill the church to overflowing.

On July 25, 1979, representatives of the clergy and laity of the Beijing diocese elected Msgr Michael Fu Tieshan[1] as bishop of the diocese, in a tradition which goes back to 1958. He was consecrated on December 21. The church gate bears the nameplate of the Patriotic Society of Chinese Catholics, the self-governing association of Chinese Catholics.

Chinese and foreign Catholics can also attend Sunday mass at St. Joseph's, popularly known as the Dongtang (East Church) in North Wangfu Street. The building itself dates back to 1905, and stands on a site where Adam Schall once lived.

The Mishitang (Rice Market Church)

The main Protestant church in Beijing is the Mishitang, at 21 North Dongdan Street; North Dongdan Street was formerly known as Mishijie (Rice Market Street), which gave the church its name. The three-storeyed building is of grey bricks in western style, with a double-eaved wooden roof in Chinese style, and dates back to the twenties, when it was founded as the headquarters of the Chinese Bible Society. Since 1958 it has been occupied by the Beijing branch of the Chinese Christian Council and the Chinese Christian Triple Independence Movement (proclaiming the independence of the Chinese Church in government, support and propagation). On the second floor is a library, services are held on the first floor, and on the ground floor are the administrative office and reception room. Sunday services are also held in the reception room now due to lack of space on the first floor.

[1]傅铁山。

Before 1958, most Protestant and Anglican denominations were represented in Beijing by missions from Britain, America, Norway, Holland and other countries. Among the most important were the Church of England, Presbyterians, Lutherans, Methodists, Congregationalists and Salvation Army. There were altogether more than sixty churches, some with very small congregations and premises. In 1958 they were amalgamated into a single body called the Chinese Christian Council.

From 1966 to 1971, during the early period of the "cultural revolution", all religious activities at the Mishitang were halted. The church was reopened on Christmas Day, 1971. Now, both Chinese and foreign Protestants in Beijing come to worship here. Worship services are held on Sundays, along with prayer-meetings on Thursday mornings, Youth Fellowship meetings on Friday evenings and evening services on Saturdays. There are four pastors attached to the church who make parish visits and perform marriages, funerals and baptisms. They also receive visiting Christians from Hongkong, Macao and abroad.

The Gangwashitang (Crock and Tile Market Church)

The Gangwashitang is at 57 South Xisi Street in the western district of Beijing. The large church can accommodate five hundred worshippers, and contains an office, chapel and baptismal font. The church was built at the beginning of the twentieth century to house the London Missionary Society. Since the merger of 1958, it has been part of the Chinese Christian Council, and its formal name is now the Gangwashi Protestant Church of Beijing. Like the Mishitang, it was closed during the "cultural revolution". After undergoing repairs it was reopened on July 13, 1980.

Four pastors are attached to the church, and worship services are held every Sunday. There are also Bible classes on Tuesday evenings and prayer-meetings on Thursday mornings. The congregation consists of both Chinese and foreign Christians.

8

The Great Wall

More than fifty kilometres northwest of Beijing is a stretch of the famous Great Wall of China. The road leads past the ancient Juyongguan (Dwelling-in-Harmony Pass) and up to the fort of Badaling (Eight Prominent Peaks), where a magnificent view of the wall is enjoyed by large numbers of Chinese and foreign visitors.

The Great Wall is a gigantic defensive project whose beginnings can be traced as far back as the 7th century B.C. At that time the rival feudal kingdoms of central and northern China built walls around their territories for self-protection. The high walls and fortresses constructed by three kingdoms, Qin, Zhao and Yan, around the 4th century B.C. as a defence against the nomadic tribes further north, laid the foundations of the present Great Wall.

Following unification of the separate kingdoms under Qin Shihuang (First Emperor of the Qin) in 221 B.C., the existing fortifications were linked up and extended. Starting from Linzhao[1] (modern Minxian,[2] Gansu) it passed through modern Inner Mongolia, Shaanxi, Shanxi and Hebei to the eastern part of Liaoning. As the

[1]临洮；[2]岷县。

crow flies this is about 2,000 kilometres, but the wall wound over high mountain ranges and valleys, and at some strategic passes, doubled back or redoubled, so that its total length is more than 5,000 kilometres. Since the latter figure is equivalent to more than 10,000 Chinese *li* the Great Wall is known in Chinese as the Ten-Thousand-*Li* Long Wall. The Qin Great Wall was located to the north of the present wall. The construction of such an immense engineering project over such difficult terrain was an extraordinary feat for ancient times. Qin Shihuang employed a workforce of almost a million, composed of soldiers, peasants and convicts, representing a fifth of the whole labour force of the country at that time. Severe hardships and back-breaking toil brought death to many of its labourers, and there are many tragic stories dating back to the time of Qin Shihuang which have become widely-known folk tales and legends.

Subsequent dynasties continued to strengthen and extend the wall. During the Han dynasty about 500 kilometres was added to the west, bringing the wall to modern Jiuquan[1] and Dunhuang[2] in Gansu. Up to the 6th century the wall continued to be an important barrier against invasion by nomadic tribes to the north. With the expansion of the Tang empire, the frontier was pushed further north, and the wall ceased to have any real function. The Jin dynasty constructed a massive system of earth works to check the advance of the Mongols, and remains of their Great Wall can still be found in Heilongjiang and Inner Mongolia. The Mongols, however, burst through the fortifications and established their own dynasty, the Yuan, to rule over China in 1280.

[1]酒泉; [2]敦煌。

In 1368, Zhu Yuanzhang drove the Mongol Yuan rulers
from the throne and established the Ming dynasty with
its capital in Nanjing. To secure his northern territories
from the remnant Mongol forces, in the very first year
of his reign he sent his senior general Xu Da to build up
the wall at Juyongguan and other strategic places. The
whole project took two hundred years to complete. The
old wall made of stones and clay was largely replaced
with a construction of evenly-sized stone blocks and
bricks. Along the wall many beacon towers were erected, to warn of an enemy's advance with smoke during
the day and fire at night. The Ming Great Wall was
12,700 *li* long, and stretched from the Yalu River[1] in Liaoning in the east to Jiayuguan[2] in Gansu in the west.
At several places the wall was redoubled for greater
protection. The section between Shanhaiguan[3] (Mountain and Sea Pass) in Hebei and the Yalu River has suffered serious damage because of its rather primitive
construction, but the rest was built very solidly and remains in reasonably good condition even today. The
Qing dynasty which practised a policy of conciliation
and amalgamation in regard to the northern territories,
did not carry out major reconstruction, and what we see
today is essentially a Ming legacy. After Liberation, the
wall was restored at three famous points, Shanhaiguan,
Badaling and Jiayuguan, where it is now a major tourist
attraction.

The Ming Great Wall averages 7.8 metres in height,
and is 6.5 metres wide at the base and 5.5 metres wide at
the top.

The section of the wall near Juyongguan and Badaling is typical of Ming construction. The wall here is high

[1]鸭绿江, [2]嘉裕关, [3]山海关。

and solid. The way along the top is paved with square bricks and provides a flat level surface, wide enough to accommodate six horses abreast. Steps have been placed where the inclination is particularly steep. The outer parapet is crenellated with merlons almost two metres high. The crenels are used as peepholes. Below the crenel on each merlon is an embrasure from which to fire at the enemy. The parapet on the inner wall is one metre high. At intervals along the inner wall are arched entrances with stairways leading to the top of the wall.

Beyond the wall at regular intervals are beacon towers. Most stand on hilltops or other easily visible sites, and some are at quite a distance from the wall. By transmitting messages by smoke signals or fire to the capital and the major garrisons, the beacon towers formed a complete communications system. During the Ming dynasty, whenever a fire or smoke signal was sent, one or more warning shot were fired simultaneously. According to the regulations issued in 1468, a single shot and a single fire or smoke signal warned that the enemy was about a hundred strong, two shots and two signals warned of five hundred, three shots and three signals warned of over a thousand and so on. In this way a message could be transmitted over more than five hundred kilometres within a few hours.

Juyongguan (Dwelling-in-Harmony Pass) and Yuntai (Cloud Terrace)

Along the line of the Great Wall are many strategic passes. One of the most important is Juyongguan, one of the nine famous fortifications of ancient China, which commands the narrow valley giving access through the

mountains to Beijing. It has two outposts, Nankou (Southern Entry) to the south and Badaling pass to the north.
Nankou, formerly a walled and fortified trading post,
leads into Guangou (Pass Ravine), a strategic valley more
than 20 kilometres long. An extra engine is needed to
push the train up the slope to the ridge above the valley.
On either side of the valley are high peaks covered with
wild flowers and undergrowth. Eight hundred years ago
this valley was one of the famous "Eight Views of Yanjing". In 1972 a wall painting was found in Eastern Han
dynasty tomb excavated in Horinger, Inner Mongolia,
which was entitled "Juyongguan" and depicted the flourishing trade that took place even then in the area around
the pass.

On either side of Juyongguan are two high mountains, and the fortress itself was situated in the narrow
gorge between them. In the centre of the pass is an
elevated stone platform called the Yuntai (Cloud Terrace). Originally it was probably the plinth of a gate-
tower, the upper part of which has collapsed. All that
is left is a balustraded terrace above an arched passageway, covered with carvings dating back to the Yuan.
The platform is also known as the Guojieta (Pagoda over
the Road), since it has also been conjectured that the terrace was originally the base of a pagoda. The terrace
rests on a broad base which narrows towards the top.
On the terrace are the remains of four stone pillars, and
the balustrade and corner posts are richly decorated with
dragon heads, wreathes and so on. The most important
carvings are concentrated on the border around the
archway and the interior of the passageway, which is
large enough to allow the passage of carriages and horses.
The border of the arch, which is shaped like half of a

hexagon, has a symmetrical pattern of crossed *vajra* (the demon-quelling "diamond mace"), with elephants, wreath-headed dragons, seven-headed dragon kings, and in the centre, a king of the birds with gold wings. On the walls inside are four very lively bas-relief carvings of the devaraja. The carvings have high artistic value, and are also very unusual in that the surface is composed of stone blocks rather than a single slab of stone.

Between the devaraja are inscriptions of *dharani* (charms) in Sanskrit, Tibetan, Xixia, Uygur and Han. The passages in the different languages are symmetrically arranged but each has a different text. It is also rare to have inscriptions in so many languages. On the ceiling of the passageway are carvings of many small Buddhas, and in the centre is a *mandala* pattern. On all sides are carvings of flowers and plants. Altogether the work is a masterpiece of Yuan stone carving.

Badaling (Eight Prominent Peaks) and the Bronze Statue of Zhan Tianyou[1]

Eleven kilometres away from Juyongguan is its northern outpost, the Badaling pass. At the pass is a small square fortress built under the Ming which is connected by its east and west gates to the Great Wall. This stretch of the wall runs in a northwesterly direction over mountain peaks and ranges.

At the Badaling train station is a bronze statue of the celebrated engineer Zhan Tianyou (1860-1919). Near it is a tablet recording his achievement in constructing the railway here under conditions of extreme difficulty.

[1]詹天佑。

BADALING AND JUYONGGUAN

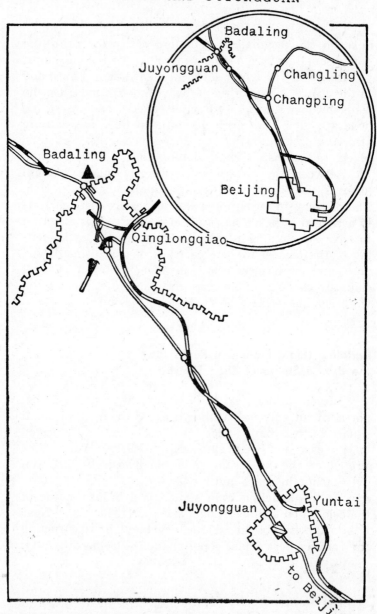

Zhan was from Nanhai, Guangdong. At the age of twelve he was sent by the Qing government to study in America, and graduated from Yale University at the age of 21. On his return to China he was first a teacher before being appointed as the chief engineer in charge of design and building of the Beijing-Zhangjiakou Railway. The stretch of railway between Nankou and Badaling passed through an extremely hazardous terrain of steep cliffs and deep valleys. At that time British and American engineers refused to take on the project claiming it was an impossible task. Zhan Tianyou, however, accepted the responsibility and the work began in 1905. Overcoming many obstacles he finally completed the work in 1909.

Passing south of the statue, the highway makes a sudden ascent, and the Great Wall comes into sight along the crest of the mountains. On the cliff face in front, someone from the ancient past has written two words "Tian Xian" (Natural Barrier), since at that time it was extremely difficult to pass or attack at this point. Beyond a narrow valley is a gate with a tablet inscribed "Outpost to Juyong": this is the entrance to the fort at Badaling, the northern outpost of Juyongguan. On the platform over the gate is a stone on which people can stand and look through a telescope to see the Baita (White Dagoba) in Beihai Park. It is called "View-of-the-Capital Stone".

From its elevated position much higher than Juyongguan, the Badaling fort is an important outpost for the defence of the pass; if it were seized, Juyongguan would be hard to defend. It was said that "the pass at Juyong is not on the Great Wall but at Badaling", and a garrison was established here for this reason.

Along the Badaling section of the Great Wall are stone steles dating from the Ming, which record the methods used to build the wall. Peasants and soldiers from all over the country were conscripted to serve in local groups each headed by an officer from the same locality; each group was responsible for a certain section of the wall, and afterwards the separate sections were joined together. Looking east from Badaling one can see at intervals several mounds and earthen walls: the mounds are the beacons described above and the walls act as a defensive line for the outpost.

Inside the gate, on the northern side of the railway, is a brick-walled fortress, the command post of Badaling. The wall, built in 1571, is ten metres high, and more than one kilometre in circumference. According to the records, there were three officers, 788 men, 23 horses and a great quantity of arms, showing the importance of the fortress at that time. The west gate is connected at both ends with the Great Wall, and has an inscription reading "The Northern Strategic Gate".

The Great Wall was not only an immense defensive edifice, but also served as an important path of communication through northern China. It also serves as a valuable museum of military life and battle conditions in ancient China. Such is its extraordinary world-wide fame that even in the depths of winter or the fiercest heat of summer, the stream of tourists never stops.

9

"The Home of Peking Man" and Lugouqiao

On the southwestern outskirts of Beijing are two famous sites rich in archeological and historical significance. Fifty kilometres from the capital is Zhoukoudian, where Peking Man lived some 500,000 years ago on Dragon Bone Hill. On the way to Zhoukoudian is Lugouqiao, known to the West as Marco Polo Bridge, and famous both for its structure and as the starting-point of the War of Resistance Against Japan in 1937.

"The Home of Peking Man"

Measuring 190 metres from east to west and 220 metres from north to south, Dragon Bone Hill has since the Ming dynasty been a limestone quarry where animal fossil bones were frequently unearthed. The local people believed these fossils to be "dragon bones", and so the hill got its name. On the northern slope of the hill is a giant natural cave: this is the "home" of Peking Man (*Homo erectus Pekinensis*), a type of early man from the Pleistocene age.

About 450 million years ago, the Zhoukoudian area was under a vast expanse of sea. A sediment of calcareous rocks accumulated on the sea floor, which later became dry land when the sea vanished as a result of the movement of the earth's crust. In the course of the ages this land was subjected to constant and corrosive erosion by rain, and gradually was reduced into a group of individual hills, one of which was Dragon Bone Hill. Water and other natural forces gradually shaped the limestone, forming crevices and caves.

Beginning some half a million years ago, Peking Man lived intermittently in one of these caves for 300,000 years, leaving behind a great quantity of discarded food, used tools and some of his own remains. As time went on, mud and sand invaded the cave and rocks broke loose, bit by bit, to complete the burial of all these remnants. During the later period of Peking Man's activities around Zhoukoudian, the cave roof collapsed and the cavity was mostly filled by mud, sand and pebbles.

In 1921, the eminent Swedish geologist, J. G. Andersson, discovered an abundance of paleo-fossils at this site. The news drew many scientists to the place, and from 1921 to 1923 their preliminary excavations uncovered many mammalian fossils, including two human teeth believed to belong to primitive man. Up to this time, there had been only two discoveries in the world of human fossils dating from around 500,000 years ago, Java Man in Indonesia (discovered 1891-1892) and Heidelberg Man in Germany (1907). Therefore this finding in Asia aroused worldwide interest.

From 1927 on, continuous excavations lasting over a period of 10 years took place at Zhoukoudian. A team of international scientists, including the Chinese paleo-anthropologist, Pei Wenzhong,[1] discovered the first complete Peking Man skullcap. On the eve of the Pacific

[1]裴文中。

The Great Wall.

Ruins of a beacon tower beyond the Great Wall.

Watch tower, crenellated parapet and embrasures.

The Yuntai (Cloud Terrace) at Juyongguan (Dwelling-in-Harmony Pass), one of the key defensive passes to Beijing.

Inscriptions of *dharani* in Sanskrit, Tibetan, Xixia, Uyghur, Mongolian and Han on the walls of the passageway under the Yuntai.

The site at Zhoukoudian where the first skull of Peking Man
was discovered in 1929.

Skull of Peking Man discovered on November 26, 1936.

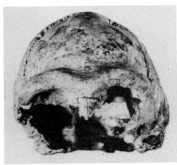

Lugouqiao (Marco Polo Bridge), the oldest stone arch bridge still in existence in north China.

Stone lions in various postures o the balusters of Lugouqiao.

This white marble stone tablet, carved with the inscription "The Moon over Lugou" by the Qing emperor Qianlong, is one of "the eight scenic spots in Beijing".

the camel, which subsisted in arid zones; the robust macaque, tiger, leopard and lion which took to dense tropical forests, and the horse, antelope and deer which roved the plains. Scientists have concluded that this variety shows there were several fluctuations in Peking Man's natural environment over several hundred thousand years.

There are more than 20 sites similar to that of Peking Man scattered on and around Dragon Bone Hill. One of the most important is the site of Upper Cave Man, situated near the crest of the hill. Morphologically speaking, Upper Cave Man was already Homo sapiens, little different from Modern Man. It is calculated that Upper Cave Man lived about 18,000 years ago, in the lower Pleistocene Epoch. From 1933 to 1934, the remains of eight individuals, including 3 complete skulls, were found there. Upper Cave Man's technical attainments are best reflected in another finding, an 83 mm-long bone needle, sharp and smooth, with a tiny eye. Made from a piece of animal bone, the needle had to be scraped, perforated and polished painstakingly. It was used to make garments from animal skins or to knot fishnets. Upper Cave Man also had personal adornments, including necklaces made from clam shells, animal teeth, or stone beads pierced and strung together.

Zhoukoudian is now one of China's major national sites under state protection. A display centre was founded there in 1953, and in 1955 a highway from Beijing was built, making access to Zhoukoudian easier. A new exhibition hall was erected in 1971. The exhibition includes replicas of the fossils of Peking Man, Upper Cave Man and various animals. Today it is visited by many tourists from both at home and abroad.

Lugouqiao (Marco Polo Bridge)

Thirty-five kilometres from the archeological site of Peking Man is Lugouqiao (Reed Gully Bridge), the arched stone bridge admired by the Italian traveller Marco Polo 700 years ago. Located 15 kilometres southwest of Beijing, it is named for the river which it spans, once known as the Lugou, now the Yongding. It is one of the longest ancient stone arch brigdes still existing in north China.

Since ancient times, the Lugouqiao area has been vital to communications between north and south and also has great military significance. Before the present bridge was built, a small wooden bridge and pontoon spanned the river. In 1153, when the Jin dynasty set up its capital in what is now the southwestern district of Beijing, it found the existing bridges could not meet its needs, and plans for a new bridge were laid. Construction began in 1189 and was completed in 1193.

The present structure is 266.5 metres long, 7.5 metres wide and supported by 11 arches. On each side of the bridge is a balustrade, and on each of its 140 balusters is a white marble lion, no two exactly alike. By the time it reaches the bridge the river current is very swift, having coursed through high mountains and deep valleys in its upper reaches. The bridge was therefore built very solidly. Its piers and arches are linked by iron bracings so that it can even resist the turbulent flood waters in spring. Though it is already over 700 years old, the load-bearing capacity of the bridge is still substantial; in a test in 1975, a 429-ton flatbed truck passed over it safely.

Owing to its solidity, the bridge has never been rebuilt, although it has undergone some renovations. Its frame, foundation, basic structural components and main carvings are mainly a legacy of the Jin dynasty. Only the bridge surface, now paved, and some of the stone carvings, balusters and lions are later restorations; although the original style and form has been preserved, nevertheless the differences from one age to another can still be discerned.

The construction of the bridge's piers is quite unusual: the side of each pier which faces upstream is pointed and topped by a triangular iron platform, with the point facing out. The point protects the bridge like a sword, parting the waters or breaking up the ice in winter. A beautiful legend has been woven about these "swords". One day several hundred years ago, the sky suddenly became overcast. Black clouds loomed up, thunder and lightning played, and the rain came pouring down. Ten fierce dragons surged down with the flood waters, destroying all in their path. Everyone was very worried that the bridge would collapse and the fields would be flooded. But as soon as they came under the bridge, the dragons disappeared, and the flood became tractable as it passed through the arches. People said it was the "swords" that killed the ferocious dragons and pacified the waters.

Visitors to the bridge seem to delight in counting the lions. There is a saying in Beijing which goes: "The lions on Lugouqiao are impossible to count," because they are too numerous. In fact, it is easy to count the big lions; it is just difficult to enumerate the small lions around the big ones. The bigger of the small ones are over 10 centimetres, but the smaller ones are only a few centimetres. The small ones seem to be playing hide-

and-seek around the feet of the big ones, and can be easily missed. In all, there are 485 lions on the bridge, 287 big and 198 small. Because of periodic renovations, the stone from which the lions are made varies. Most of the lions have been restored since the 14th century, and few of those carved in the 12th and 13th centuries remain.

The Lugouqiao lions are extremely life-like, whether shown rampant or couchant. Some have their chests thrust forth to gaze at the sky; some stare with fixed attention at the bridge; some turn their heads to face their neighbour as if to chat; some fondle their cubs, appearing to call them softly. On one baluster at the southeast end of the bridge is a lion with an ear pricked up, which seems to be listening intently to the sounds of the water underneath and the conversation of the people passing by.

At each end of the bridge are two *huabiao* (carved ornamental columns), similar to the *huabiao* in front of Tiananmen. The *huabiao* are 4.65 metres high, and rest on a stone pedestal. Beside the *huabiao* at each end are a white marble stele pavilion and an additional stele resting on a turtle; the northern stele has an inscription by Kangxi and the southern stele has one by Qianlong.

The best time to visit the bridge is said to be in the dawn moonlight. From the bridge one can see the river stretching like a girdle across the fields. In the first rays of the morning sun, the Western Hills outside Beijing appear and recede from view. "The morning moon over Lugou" is one of the "Eight Views of Yanjing", and has been celebrated in prose and verse by many travellers and writers.

In addition to its historic, scientific and artistic value, the bridge has a further claim to fame as the site of the "July 7 Lugouqiao Incident". It was here that on July 7, 1937, Japan fired the first shot that began the full-scale war of invasion against China. Under the leadership of the Chinese Communist Party, the Chinese people waged the War of Resistance Against Japan which lasted eight years (1937-1945). Marks left by the Japanese bullets and artillery bombardments still can be seen on the bridge and on the city wall of Wanping at the eastern end of the bridge. Thus, Lugouqiao is of double significance: an historical monument and revolutionary memorial.

10

Museums and Libraries

Beijing is not only an ancient capital but also the cultural centre of new China. Besides the Palace Museum and the Museums of the Chinese Revolution and Chinese History which have been described in earlier chapters, there are several other museums and also the country's biggest library. Two lesser-known museums, an observatory and two libraries are described in this chapter.

The Lu Xun Museum

This museum, which commemorates China's outstanding writer of this century, Lu Xun, is located to the North Inner Fuchengmen Street, adjoining one of Lu Xun's former residence. The museum was founded in 1956 on the 20th anniversary of his death and expanded in 1981, on the centenary of his birth.

In addition to being a brilliant writer, Lu Xun was a leading figure in contemporary Chinese history, a pioneer in the twentieth century movement for a liberal and democratic China. Although he lived only 56 years, he produced a great quantity of work. *Lu Xun Quanji* (Complete Works of Lu Xun) and *Lu Xun Yiwenji* (Translated Works of Lu Xun), published in 1956 to commemorate the 20th anniversary of his death, consists of 20 volumes of works and translations totalling more than six million characters and a 16-volume new edition of *Lu Xun Quanji* appeared in 1981, centenary of his birth. The first introduction of his works to foreign readers was in 1926, when "The True Story of Ah Q" was translated into French and carried in the May and June issues of *Europe*. "This is a realistic, masterful work, explicit and rich in satire.... Ah Q's pitiful image will long remain in people's memory," commented Romain Rolland.

Lu Xun's real name was Zhou Shuren.[1] He was born on September 25, 1881, in Shaoxing,[2] Zhejiang. His father, Zhou Boyi,[3] was a scholar who died young. Lu Xun later wrote an essay entitled "Father's Illness", venting his anger at the murdering ignorant doctors who had treated his father with medicines like broken-drum-boluses and original pairs of mating crickets. Clearly, it was his bitterly keen insight into the backwardness, ignorance and corruption of the old China that drove Lu Xun to seek for a new remedy to cure the old society.

During the writer's adolescence, misfortune befell his family. His grandfather was put in jail and the family was reduced to poverty. A regular customer at the pawnshop, Lu Xun became an object of disdain and was often scolded as a beggar. As he once wrote, "the true face of his fellow man" was laid bare before him.

It was common for scholars of Lu Xun's time to study the Chinese classics, take the imperial examinations and receive official appointments. Lu Xun lacked the money to take this road, nor had he any desire to be a merchant or the private secretary to an official. But

[1]周树人； [2]绍兴； [3]周伯宜。

it happened to be a time when the Qing government was carrying out a programme for Westernization, and so Lu Xun went to Nanjing in 1898 for a Western-style education. After graduation, Lu Xun was awarded a government scholarship to study in Japan. His experience abroad exposed him to new sciences, new civilizations and new ideas, and prompted him to begin to explore ways to save his nation.

Lu Xun lived in Japan from 1902 to 1909. Then and later Lu Xun developed close ties with Japan, and found many good friends and teachers among the Japanese. Nevertheless as a student from the weak and corrupt Qing Empire, he suffered very deeply. When he was studying medicine in Sendai, each time he passed an exam he would be accused of cheating, because nobody would believe that the imbecile Chinese were capable of academic achievement. Once Lu Xun was watching a newsreel, amid the cheers of the Japanese students, in which Japanese troops were executing a Chinese as a Russian spy; the onlookers were also Chinese. Deeply shocked, Lu Xun abandoned medicine and left Sendai for Tokyo. He had decided to devote himself to the task of breaking through this terrible apathy and arousing his fellow-countrymen to make China strong. Literature was to be his means.

Lu Xun returned to China in 1909 and started teaching first in Hangzhou and then in Shaoxing. Soon the bourgeois revolution of 1911, led by Dr. Sun Yat-sen, broke out. Lu Xun welcomed the new republic with great hope and in 1912 he assumed a post in the Ministry of Education under the provisional government in Nanjing. In May that year he moved with the rest of the Ministry to Beijing, where he lived for 14 years. Here he witnessed the failure of the 1911 Revolution, and his bitter disappointment led to frustration and dejection. For many years he lived alone in the Shaoxing Hostel in Nanbanbi *hutong* outside Xuanwumen, copying ancient stone tablet inscriptions, compiling classical texts, studying history and culture and analyzing Chinese society and revolution.

In 1919 the anti-imperialist and anti-feudal May 4th Movement broke out. It was part of a larger "New Cultural Movement" in which Lu Xun was a pioneer. His first short story, "A Madman's Diary",[1] was published in 1918, revealing the cannibalistic feudal ethics that had prevailed in China for 5,000 years. This short story ushered in the new literature of contemporary China.

From this time on he wrote prolifically. His short stories from this period were collected into two volumes, *Call to Arms*[2] (1922) and *Wandering*[3] (1926), and his essays formed several volumes. In 1920 he began to lecture first at Beijing University and later at seven other colleges as well. His lecture notes were published as *An Outline History of Chinese Fiction*[4] (1923-24), still a classic of Chinese literary history.

His activities having aroused the enmity of the warlord government of that time, Lu Xun was forced to leave Beijing in August 1926 and joined the faculties of first Xiamen University and later Sun Yat-sen University in Guangzhou. Soon after his move to Guangzhou, Chiang Kai-shek[5] put an end to the period of Kuomintang cooperation with the Communist Party of China and instituted a massacre of Communists and revolutionaries. Lu Xun left Guangzhou for Shanghai in September 1927. In Shanghai he took a house with a former pupil, Xu

[1]《狂人日记》；[2]《呐喊》；[3]《彷徨》；[4]《中国小说史略》；[5]蒋介石。

Guangping;[1] he was nearly 50 when he began to enjoy the happiness of family life. Two years later his son Hai-ying was born.

In Shanghai, he became one of the leaders of the new Left-wing cultural movement. It was a very productive period for him, with almost one collection of essays appearing each year. From an ideological and artistic point of view, his works of the thirties showed more maturity, penetration and erudition than his earlier ones. In this period, Lu Xun also supported the new woodcut movement and compiled several picture albums. A lover of art since childhood, Lu Xun often designed his own book jackets.

During his 10 years in Shanghai, Lu Xun was compelled by the Kuomintang "white terror" to exist semi-underground, and he sometimes even had to leave home. His works were banned and he was obliged to keep changing the penname under which he wrote. It has been calculated that throughout his lifetime he used 128 different pennames. The difficult conditions and his arduous work aggravated his tuberculosis and his health seriously deteriorated. On October 19, 1936 he passed away in Shanghai.

With a contingent of Chiang Kai-shek's secret agents and foreign concession policemen watching them, 20,000 people of all social strata gathered together spontaneously in Shanghai to hold a funeral for their beloved writer. The coffin was covered with a white silk banner, which bore three gleaming black characters, "Soul of the Nation", the highest tribute the people could give to a writer.

Aside from his Chinese friends, Lu Xun had many

[1]许广平。

friends from Europe, North America and Japan. They included Uchiyama Kanzo, Kaji Wataru and Masuda Wataru, Yamamoto Hatsue, the Russian poet, Vasily Eroshenko, and the American journalists, Agnes Smedley and Edgar Snow. When George Bernard Shaw visited Shanghai in 1933, Lu Xun lunched with him at Soong Ching Ling's[1] residence, an occasion commemorated in a well-known photograph, and wrote several essays about him afterwards. Lu Xun also admired Käthe Kollwitz, a German graphic artist whose work he tried to introduce to China, and compiled a collection of her lithographs during his last illness.

During his lifetime, Lu Xun translated more than 200 works by more than ninety writers from 14 countries, totalling over 2.5 million characters and making up nearly half of the 20 volumes of his *Complete Works*. The authors include Gogol, Chekhov, Gorki, Heine, Nietzsche, Jules Verne, Petöfi, Mickiewicz, Kuriyagawa Hakuson, Natsume Soseki and Fadeyev, writers and literary theorists from East and West, past and present. When Lu Xun's "The True Story of Ah Q" came out in French, few people outside China had ever heard of its author. Since then Lu Xun's works have been published in more than 30 countries in over 50 languages, and he has a growing following the world over.

Although nearly half a century has elapsed since Lu Xun died, his memory has not been forgotten. Many places in Shaoxing, Beijing, Guangdong and Shanghai where he once worked and lived have been restored, and museums and memorial halls have been established.

The Beijing Lu Xun Museum has amassed a large

[1]宋庆龄。

body of material by and about Lu Xun; over 1,000 pages of manuscripts of poems and essays, over 1,100 letters, more than 1,400 pages of old records edited by him, and about 1,000 pages of his diary from 1912 to the day before his death (altogether 25 years, minus entries for 1922 which were lost because of war). Lu Xun's manuscripts are mostly written with a Chinese brush, in a neat, clear hand. His longest manuscript is the Chinese translation of Gogol's *Dead Souls*; the shortest are poems with five or seven characters to a line. Among the earliest manuscripts at the museum is a letter Lu Xun wrote to Jiang Yizhi in October 1904, while the last is "A Few Matters Connected with Zhang Taiyan" written only two days before his death. The article "The Origin of Fire" and some letters to one of his Japanese friends, Uchiyama Kanzo, are in Japanese.

The museum also holds many scrolls on which Lu Xun wrote poems for his friends, such as "Saying from *Laozi*" and "Tang Qianqi's 'Returning Wild Goose'", given to Nagao Kagekazu and Ohara Eigiro. These are not only witness to Lu Xun's friendship with Japanese people but are also artistically valuable examples of calligraphy.

Lu Xun was extremely fond of his own library and the museum still houses 13,000 books of his. He repaired many of his own books himself and a set of his bindery tools is now on display. There are several thousand other articles left behind by Lu Xun, including some of his clothes and items used in daily life, textbooks from his early studies, anatomy notes from his medical school days in Sendai, with handwritten corrections by his teacher, Mr. Fujino, and lecture notes from his course on the history of Chinese fiction at Beijing University in 1920.

To the west of the museum is a small house in traditional Chinese courtyard style where Lu Xun lived from May 1924 to August 1926. In its two neat courtyards are two date trees, and the purple and white lilac bushes that Lu Xun planted in the yard half a century ago are still flourishing.

The three rooms at the south are the guest rooms, and are furnished very simply. To the north are the living quarters: his mother's bedroom to the east, a living room to the west, and in the middle Lu Xun's own room, which served as both a bedroom and workroom. It is in this last "room for combat", as Lu Xun called it, that he wrote the short stories and essays he produced in those years.

After Liberation, Lu Xun's former residence was fully repaired and his possessions arranged as they were in his lifetime.

The Museum of Natural History

The Beijing Museum of Natural History, a cream-coloured building on the east side of Tianqiao Street in the southern part of the city, is an institute for popularizing scientific knowledge as well as for scientific research. Through four exhibition halls dealing with plants, animals, prehistoric animals and primitive man, the museum explains the development of inanimate objects to organisms, lower organisms to higher organisms and ape to man.

Specimens of modern plants and ancient plant fossils are displayed in the Botany Hall, which presents the main categories and evolution of plants. The exhibit goes back to 1,800,000,000-600,000,000 years ago, when the first algae emerged, the stramatolites of the Sinian Period followed by the pteridophytes. Samples of herbaceous pteridophytes which still exist are on display, as well as fossils from ancient pteridophytes. Next comes the development of the gymnosperms, which flourished in the Mesozoic Era (222,000,000-70,000,000 years ago) and afterwards declined; modern gymnosperms include the gingko and metasequois. Last come the angiosperms, the highest form of flora with the most varieties (about 200,000); they provide food and clothing for mankind, enabling human society to flourish.

The Zoology Hall shows the milestones in the evolution of animals from the unicellular to the first multicellular invertebrates and thence to vertebrates. Invertebrates on display include sponges, colelenterates, flat-worms, cyclostomes, annelids, mollusca, arthropods and echinoderms. Among them are strange and colourful specimens of coral, shellfish, shrimp, crab and insects.

Vertebrates on display include representative specimens from the five main categories, fish, amphibians, reptiles, birds and mammals. Among the rare species unique to China shown here are the psephurus gladius and myxocyprinus asiaticus (fish); the Chinese salmander (amphibian); the Yangtze River crocodile (reptile); the crossoptilon mantchuricum, golden pheasant, and peacock (bird); and the giant panda, golden monkey, takin and liptotes vexillifer (mammal).

The Paleozoology Hall displays fossils of ancient vertebrates, showing vertebrate evolution from aquatic to terrestrial, cold-blooded to warm-blooded, and oviparous to viviparous. Fossils collected from all over China illustrate the transitional periods; for instance, fossils of multi-gilled fish and Yunnan fish from Yunnan give insight into evolution of fish in the Devonian Period, and Rana basaltica (Young) and procynops mioceneus show amphibian development.

The museum display includes extensive and valuable fossils of the reptilian dinosaurs unearthed after China's Liberation in 1949. On display is a skeleton of the "giant of the animal kingdom", the dinosaur of Mamenxi Village, Mamenchisaurus Constructus Young, unearthed in Hechuan, Sichuan, 22 metres long and 3.5 metres tall, which lived on plants in the late Jurassic Period. Also on display are the remains of the largest duck-billed dinosaur in the world, 8 metres tall and 15 metres long; known as the "huge Shandong dinosaur", or Tsintaosaurus Spinorhinus Young, it lived in the late Cretaceous Period. Aquatic and flying reptiles are represented by the Zhungel Pterodactyl unearthed in Xinjiang, northwest China, with a wing span of more than two metres that lived in the late Cretaceous Period, and the Himalayan Ichthyosaur unearthed in Tibet, whose discovery has proved that today's "roof of the world" was under an ocean during the same period. Other exhibits include fossils of the nine Parakannemeyeria Brevirostrit representing a branch of evolution which came to a dead-end; ancient mammal fossils dating from the Paleocene Period discovered in Guangdong, Anhui, Hunan and Xinjiang; rather complete skeletons of the bemalambadid from Guangdong; fossils of rodent dinosaurs, carnivores, artiodactyls, primates, elephant bones and skulls, the most striking being from the Yellow River stegodon unearthed in Heshui, Gansu, which is eight metres long and four metres tall, and the most complete fossil of a stegodon unearthed anywhere in the world.

The Paleoanthropology Hall shows how mankind began and developed. The remains of humans found in China such as Yuanmou Man, Lantian Man, Peking Man, Tingtsun Man, Upper Cave Man, Panpo Man and Lungshan (Dragon Hill) Man are included in the display, along with models of related finds abroad such as Homohabillis, Java Man, Homo Neanderthalensis and Cro-magnon Man. Dioramas depict Peking Man and Upper Cave Man at labour.

Beijing Observatory

In the eastern part of Beijing, just southwest of a new highway flyover at Jianguomen, is a high platform bearing an array of large bronze astronomical instruments. This is the ancient Beijing observatory whose origins date from the Ming dynasty.

According to historical records, there were astronomical instruments and an observatory in Beijing as early as in the Jin dynasty. In 1127, when Jin troops occupied Bianjin (now Kaifeng in Henan), capital of the Northern Song dynasty, they shipped many historical relics, books and treasures to Zhongdu, the newly-built Jin capital in the southwest of modern Beijing. Among them were some Song astronomical instruments, which were later installed on a platform set up by the Jin imperial court.

When the Yuan dynasty built its new capital Dadu slightly northeast of Zhongdu, astronomical observations were at first made mostly through these Song instruments on the Jin platform. In the spring of 1279, an Imperial College of Astronomy and an astronomical observatory were set up at the southeastern corner of Dadu around the site of the present observatory. A variety of astronomical instruments designed and made by the engineer Guo Shoujin and other Yuan astronomers were installed on the new observatory. Both observatory and instruments represented the highest level of astronomy in the world at that time. The Song instruments then became museum pieces and were exhibited on the Jin platform, in the southwestern suburbs of Dadu. After the fall of the Yuan dynasty in 1358, both the Song and the Yuan instruments were shipped to Nanjing, the Ming dynasty's new capital, and the old observatories temporarily fell into disuse.

In 1406, the Yongle emperor of the Ming dynasty decided to move the capital back to Beijing. In the early period of reconstruction, priority was given to palaces and city walls, and the building of observatories and other such facilities got underway only after 1436, during the Zhengtong reign. In 1437, the Board of Astronomy at the Ming court sent workers to Nanjing to make wood models of the Song armillary sphere and Yuan abridged armilla and sundial. The models were then shipped back to Beijing and cast into bronze. Over the next few years several buildings were erected to house these instruments, such as the observatory, the Ziweidian (Hall of Celestial Abstruseness) and the Guiyingtang (Sundial Hall). This observatory laid the foundations for the present building. Large-scale renovation was carried out during the Jiajing reign, but since then no major changes have been made. Some of the Jiajing bricks marked with the reign can still be found in the observatory walls.

The instruments installed on the observatory in Ming times include an armillary sphere, an abridged armilla and a celestial globe. Their main use was to take global bearings of the stars in order to compare the movements of the planets and record other celestial phenomena. At the foot of the observatory were a sundial and a clepsydra. The sundial is the earliest and simplest of all astronomical instruments, originating before writing was invented; it was used for calculating the calendar. The clepsydra was used to calculate the passage of time over the cycle of day and night.

The arrival of Jesuit missionaries in China, in the seventeenth century introduced Western astronomy into China. In 1674, during the reign of the Kangxi emperor, six large-scale bronze instruments constructed according to Western astronomical science by Father Verbiest were built and installed on the observatory: a celestial globe, an equatorial theodolite, a zodiac theodolite, an altazimuth, a quadrant and an ancient sextant. The less sophisticated Ming instruments were then moved down to the ground. In 1716, another large altazimuth in decorative Louis Quatorze style was added to the set. By now the platform was becoming somewhat crowded, and the eastern side was widened by about 5 metres. In 1745, in the Qianlong period, work began on the design and manufacture of an instrument called ji,[1] which took 10 years to complete. The ji is actually an armilla built according to Western methods. Beautifully designed and exquisitely executed, it illustrates the high technological

[1] 玑衡抚辰仪。

level of the Qing in its heyday. It was the eighth and last of the astronomical set.

In 1900, when the allied forces of the eight powers invaded Beijing, German and French troops looted all the astronomical instruments both on the platform and at its foot. Some years later, France returned some of the treasures to China under the pressure of world condemnation. Those taken away by the Germans were displayed in Potsdam, Berlin, and were returned to Beijing only in 1921 after World War I in compliance with the Versailles Peace Treaty.

On the eve of the War of Resistance Against Japan in the late 1930s, the Kuomintang authorities fled southward to Nanjing, taking with them the seven Ming instruments and leaving only the Qing pieces. The eight Qing instruments are now the only ones remaining on the observatory.

Despite the vicissitudes of the past 500 years, the Beijing Observatory has survived remarkably well. Its platform, attached buildings and 15 large astronomical instruments (including the seven still in Nanjing) have remained basically intact. Nevertheless this scientifically and historically important site has fallen into disuse and disrepair, and is not now open to the public. The instruments and foundation are now being renovated, however, and the site is expected to be reopened soon.

Beijing Library

Beijing Library, China's national library for more than 70 years, is the country's largest both in size and in number of books. It now contains more than 9.8 million volumes, documents and manuscripts, seven times as many as in 1949 (1.4 million), and 100 times as many as it had at its founding (about 90,000).

The main library building, a palace-style structure with a green glazed-tile roof, stands inside a red-walled compound to the west of Beihai Park in the centre of Beijing. Its predecessor was the Qing Imperial Library, founded in 1910 and opened to the public in 1912 after the Republican Revolution. Although as a national library it is comparatively young, much of its collection can be traced back to earlier times. For instance, it has inherited the collections of the Jixidian, the imperial library of the Southern Song dynasty, and of the Wenyuange, the imperial library of the Ming dynasty. On its founding in 1910, it incorporated the Cabinet Library, the Imperial Academy Library and the Imperial College Library from the Qing court, plus some private libraries; it subsequently acquired the *Siku Quanshu* formerly held at the Wenjinge in Chengde, manuscripts from the Dunhuang Grottoes and the library of the Yang family from Liaocheng, Shandong. Since 1949, the library has been further enriched through purchases, exchanges and gifts.

The *Siku Quanshu* (Complete Library of the Four Treasuries of Knowledge), an encyclopedic collection of premodern books compiled 200 years ago, is stored in the rare-book room. Its 3,503 titles in 36,304 volumes are divided into four categories: classics, history, philosophy and belles lettres. It is one of the only seven original manuscript copies, and is bound in traditional Chinese thread-bound style with covers of green, red, blue and grey silk. The rare-book room also houses the famous

Yongle Dadian[1] (Yongle Encyclopedia), completed 570 years ago under the Yongle emperor of the Ming dynasty. It originally consisted of 11,095 volumes in 22,937 fascicles, but most were lost in the plunder and destruction of the Western powers in 1900; only some 200 volumes are left in the Beijing Library.

There are also quite a number of books printed from wood blocks dating from the Song, Jin and Yuan dynasties (10th to 14th centuries). Among them is what may be the world's earliest bound book, *Wenyuan Yinghua*[2] (Flowers from the Literary Garden), from the Jixidian Collection in the Southern Song imperial library. The book was designed and bound by a Chinese worker named Wan Run in 1260. Others include an incomplete Song dynasty edition of *Kaibao Zang*[3] made from a block cut in 971; *Zhaocheng Zang*,[4] printed from stone blocks in 1148 under the Jin dynasty; *Mengxi Bitan*[5] (Notes from the Dream Brook) printed in 1305. *Shizhuzhai Jianpu*[6] (Designs for Letter Paper from the Studio of Ten Bamboos), printed from blocks engraved around 1644, features colour illustrations and is considered a masterpiece of Ming dynasty colour printing.

The library has a great number of other threadbound books on many subjects including philosophy, economics, politics, military affairs, literature, art, history, geography, astronomy, mathematics, chemistry, medicine, architecture and hydraulics. It also has books in the languages of more than twenty of China's minorities, including Mongolian, Manchu, Uygur and Korean.

The periodical collection has complete sets of Chinese and foreign publications, including the *Proceedings*

---

[1] 《永乐大典》；[2] 《文苑英华》；[3] 《开宝藏》；[4] 《赵城藏》；[5] 《梦溪笔谈》；[6] 《十竹斋笺谱》。

of the Royal Society of Edinburgh (1788), *Nature* (1869) and the U.S. *Chemical Abstracts* (1907). There are also fairly complete sets of some early Chinese newspapers and magazines including *Dongfang Zazhi*[1] (Eastern Miscellany) from 1904, *Minbao*[2] (People's Herald), *Shiwu*[3] (Current Affairs) and *Shenbao*[4] (Shanghai Daily).

Since 1949, the library has acquired many volumes of Marxist classics and documents of revolutionary significance.   They include originals of letters between Marx and Engels; a copy of the first German edition of *Das Kapital* published in 1867; one of the first Russian editions of Lenin's *What Is to Be Done?*; an early edition of the late Chairman Mao Zedong's *On New Democracy* printed from wood blocks; *Shao Nian*[5] (Youth), a magazine edited by the late Premier Zhou Enlai while a member of a Chinese communist student group in Paris, and many publications from China's revolutionary base areas during the war years.   Along with these in the rare-book room are original manuscripts by famous modern scholars and writers, including Lu Xun, Guo Moruo, Mao Dun and Ba Jin.

Today, Beijing Library has taken on a new look. The fifteen reading rooms with 2,000 seats are full everyday with readers ranging from grey-haired professors and specialists to young technicians, workers and students.   Five hundred and ninety thousand readers were admitted in 1978. Though its floor space has increased from the pre-Liberation 8,000 square metres to 50,000, it still cannot accommodate all those who wish to use it.   A new library building is under construction, and new reading rooms are being set up.

[1]《东方杂志》; [2]《民报》; [3]《时务》; [4]《申报》; [5]《少年》。

Beijing Library has done much to promote cultural exchange with other countries. It has exchange relations with 2,000 libraries in 120 countries and Hongkong and Macao, and librarians from Beijing Library have been on delegations visiting libraries in the United States, Japan, Australia and Britain; librarians from those countries have also visited Beijing Library.

The Capital Library

The Capital Library is located within Andingmen in the northeastern part of Beijing in the former Guozijian (Imperial College), the highest ranking college in China during the Yuan, Ming and Qing dynasties. It was founded in 1306 by the Yuan to educate the sons of high-ranking Mongolian families in the Chinese language and script, and also enrolled Chinese students to study the Mongolian language and mounted archery. It was situated due west of the Kongmiao (Temple of Confucius), also founded by the Yuan, following the convention that a school should stand to the left of a temple. At the beginning of the Ming dynasty the name was changed briefly to the Beiping Junxue (Beiping Prefectural College), but with the relocation of the Ming capital to Beijing by the Yongle emperor the old name was restored. During the Ming and Qing the college was mainly devoted to the teaching of the Confucian classics. It was enlarged by the Qianlong emperor in 1783, who ordered that the Thirteen Classics of traditional Confucianism be engraved on stone tablets as an imperishable and standard version. There are altogether 189 steles, plus one bearing the imperial edict, and about 630,000 characters inscribed by the same hand. The emperor even gave lectures here in person; on these occasions he would lead his officials and the college teachers and students in worshipping Confucius at the temple nearby.

The centrepiece of the old college is the Piyong (Sovereign Concord), built under Qianlong, where the emperor would lecture on the classics. It is a large and splendid building in a fine setting. Around it runs a gallery, and beyond is a moat with a finely-carved white marble balustrade. Four bridges lead across the moat to the four doors of the Piyong. To the north of the Piyong is the Yiluntang (Hall of Sacrifice for Ethics), the college library. Before the construction of the Piyong, the emperor gave his lectures here. (It is now a reading room.) Alongside of the Piyong are 33 rooms where the college students carried out their studies. The student dormitories which were situated near the Imperial College no longer exist. A special Russian Hostel was set up in 1728 to accommodate students sent from Russia to study here.

The Imperial College was put under special state protection as a national cultural treasure in 1956 and given a new face; that winter it was reopened as the Capital Library. The nameplate over the main gate was written by the late Guo Moruo, President of the Chinese Academy of Sciences, for the opening of the new library.

Under the administration of the Beijing municipal government, the library is an all-purpose library. Its main task is to serve scientific research and the popularization of science. A quarter of the 2,000,000 books in Chinese and foreign languages in the library are on science and technology. The library also collects local materials and documents and has amassed

some 8,000 items, so that it is an excellent source
for the study of Beijing's past. It also holds more than
30,000 rare books from the Song, Yuan, Ming and Qing
dynasties, and some famous old libraries. Its treasures
include a 1623 Ming edition of *Jingshi Tongyan*[1] (Stories
to Warn Men) and *Xingshi Hengyan*[2] (Stories to Awaken
Men), and the late Qing *Chewangfu Quben*[3] (A Mongolian
Prince's Palace Collection of Folk Literature).

[1]《警世通言》; [2]《醒世恒言》; [3]《车王府曲本》。

11

Institutes of Higher Education

About a dozen institutes of higher education, including universities, colleges, an institute of physical culture and a nationalities institute, are concentrated in the northwestern outskirts of Beijing. Some of these institutions are internationally famous for their long history, high scholarly standards and the achievements of its faculty and graduates. Three outstanding institutes are described in this chapter.

Beijing University

The Beijing University campus occupies about 145 hectares of land on the northwestern outskirts of Beijing in a beautiful park-like setting which dates back to the Qianlong reign of the Qing. The campus was founded in 1922 to house the famous American Methodist Yanjing (Yenching) University, and a modified Chinese style of architecture was adopted for its main buildings. Winding paths and streams still flow past these older buildings with their *huabiao* and stone animals standing in front, and the modern teaching centre and library were built nearby, reminders of historical change and progress. In the northwest corner of the campus is a lake reflecting the pavilions and the pagoda-style water-tower along its shore. It was never given a formal name and so became known as Weiminghu (Unnamed Lake).

Founded in the closing days of the 19th century, Beijing University is one of China's oldest educational bodies, a product of the efforts of the Guangxu emperor to carry out institutional reform and a modernization programme in 1898. Among the new schools set up to study Western learning was the Jingshi Daxuetang (Capital College), the predecessor of Beijing University, located near the centre of Beijing. When the Empress Dowager Cixi staged a coup d'état and put the Guangxu emperor under house arrest, she rescinded all the new policies and programmes. The Capital College was the only institution that survived. However, it was not a place where academic freedom was encouraged, for it was under the direct control of the Qing government. The students were either fifth to eighth grade officials or successful scholars from the upper levels of the imperial examination system. They came to school on horseback or in sedan chairs and lived the life of lordly officials.

After the 1911 Revolution the college was renamed Beijing University (usually referred to as Beida for short). When the well-known educationalist Cai Yuanpei[1] (1876-1940) was appointed chancellor in 1917, he introduced many reforms. His support for science and democracy blew a fresh wind into the depressed and lethargic campus and opened the way for new ways of thinking. People of different schools of thought expressed their views freely and held debates with one another in a lively atmosphere, and Beida grew into an ideolog-

[1] 蔡元培。

ical and cultural centre of China. Li Dazhao[1] (1888-1927), who organized the first Marxist study group in China and later became a founder of the Chinese Communist Party, was appointed the university chief librarian and professor of economics in 1918; Chen Duxiu[2] (1879-1942), who became the first general secretary of the Chinese Communist Party, was appointed Dean of the School of Liberal Arts in 1917. Lu Xun (1881-1936), the famous writer and thinker of modern China, lectured at Beida on the history of Chinese fiction in the early twenties; and Mao Zedong worked in the library from 1918 to 1919. It was at this time that Mao became acquainted with new thinking in China and at the age of 25 began to devote himself to the study of Marxism. The rooms where Mao Zedong and Li Dazhao worked are still kept intact in the Red Building at the university's former address.

Beijing University has always been in the vanguard of democratic and revolutionary movements in modern Chinese history. On May 4, 1919, hundreds of Beida students took to the streets to demonstrate against the warlord government's plans to sign the Paris Peace Treaty, which included a provision handing over Germany's former concessions in China to Japan. The angry students stormed and set fire to the mansion of Cao Rulin,[3] the Minister of Communications who was China's representative to the negotiations on Japan's "Twenty-one Demands" and had close associations with the Japanese. As a result of the protests, Cao resigned from the government and the delegates at the Peace Conference refused to sign the treaty. This anti-imperialist movement, known as the May 4th Movement, originated

[1]李大钊；[2]陈独秀；[3]曹汝霖。

at Beida and later spread to all parts of the country, marking the beginning of modern Chinese history. Beijing University students again stood at the forefront of struggle in the December 9th Movement against Chiang Kai-shek's policy of non-resistance towards the Japanese imperialists in 1935, and in the movement opposing civil war, hunger and persecution in the areas under Chiang Kai-shek's rule after World War II.

In 1952, after the establishment of new China, Beida was amalgamated with Yanjing University and took over the Yanjing campus. In the past 30 years, Beida has become one of the country's major centres of teaching and scientific research.

Beida at present has 22 departments, 66 subjects and 14 research institutes, with nearly 8,000 students in all. Millions of Chinese youngsters aspire to study at Beida. Since 1977, the number of people taking the entrance exams has been many times the number of places available, so that only the most outstanding are accepted. Of the top five students who took part in a national mathematics contest in 1977, three are now studying in the mathematics department at Beida. The two top place-getters in the arts and sciences among the 4.6 million students who took the national entrance exams in 1979 have been admitted to Beida, one in the Chinese literature department and the other in physics. The student's tuition is paid by the government, as at other institutions of higher education in China. The well-equipped university hospital provides free medical care, and government grants are available to students from poorer families.

The faculty at Beida is considered among the best in the country, and many of its 380 professors are well-known scholars. The famous demographer, Ma Yinchu,[1] who advocated planned population growth in 1957, was President of the university in the 1950s. He is now the Honorary President of Beida. On the south side of the campus behind a bamboo grove is the residence of the famous linguist, Professor Wang Li.[2] Wang Li has spent more than 50 years studying the Chinese language and has written many books and papers on Chinese phonetics, grammar, linguistic history and prosody.

Beida provides a favourable environment for scientific research. University researchers have developed the principal part for a system of laser editing and typesetting of Chinese characters, which has modernized China's printing and photo-composition.

The Beijing University library is China's largest university library. Its holdings of Chinese and foreign books amount to some 3.2 million volumes, including manuscripts from the 6th and 7th centuries, woodblock printed books from the 10th century, copper typeset books from the 17th century, ancient colour printing and early editions of the world's classics. Among its rare books are a 1103 edition of *Datang Xiyuji*[3] (Records of the Western Regions of the Great Tang) by the Buddhist monk Xuanzang,[4] and a 1760 edition of *Hongloumeng*[5] (Dream of Red Mansions) by Cao Xueqin,[6] with a commentary by Zhiyanzhai.[7]

Beida is also a famous teaching institute. Graduates from Beida and the former Yanjing University are now scattered throughout China and the world. Many of them have become outstanding scholars and statesmen. The noted geologist Li Siguang[8] was appointed head of

[1]马寅初； [2]王力； [3]《大唐西域记》； [4]玄奘； [5]《红楼梦》； [6]曹雪芹； [7]脂砚斋； [8]李四光。

the geological department in 1929. It was he who first pointed out that the continental deposit was oil bearing, repudiating the theory that China was an oil-poor country. His student, Pei Wenzhong,[1] was a member of the team which discovered the 500,000-year-old skull of Peking Man. Most of China's older generation of geologists are Beida graduates. Many famous Chinese writers are graduates of Beida, including the late Mao Dun[2] (1896-1981), Chairman of the Chinese Writers' Association, Xie Bingxin[3] (1908-) and the British writer Han Suyin.[4] On Beida's 80th anniversary in May 1978, Mao Dun wrote an emotional letter to his old school recalling his years there.

Many foreigners have taught, studied or worked at Beida, and some have become close friends of the Chinese people. The most famous of these was the American journalist Edgar Snow, author of *Red Star over China*, a book that caused a stir throughout the world. In 1934, Snow, then a correspondent for *Asia* and the *Saturday Evening Post*, was also a part-time lecturer in the department of journalism of Yanjing University. While studying Chinese and writing his dispatches, he formed a close association with the progressive students. China's present Foreign Minister Huang Hua[5] was then a leader of the Yanjing students' union, and later went to Yan-an with Snow's help. When the War of Resistance Against Japan broke out in 1937, Deng Yingchao,[6] wife of the late Premier Zhou Enlai, was recuperating from an illness in the Western Hills. Snow disguised her as his nurse to help her leave Beijing safely and avoid arrest by the enemy. Before his death, Snow asked that part of his ashes be buried in China. A site on the banks of

---

[1]斐文中；[2]茅盾；[3]谢冰心；[4]韩素音；[5]黄华；·[6]邓颖超。

the Weiminghu was chosen, and a white tombstone now marks the spot where the ashes were buried. Zhou Enlai and Deng Yingchao were present at the interment in 1973. With deep feeling, the premier said, "He will remain here. The Chinese people will never forget him."

In the thirty years since Liberation, more than 2,500 foreign students from over 50 countries have studied at Beida. The present enrollment of foreign students is around 130. Most spend at least one year studying Chinese at the Beijing Languages Institute before proceeding to university classes in Chinese literature, history, philosophy, economics, chemistry and biology.

Qinghua (Tsinghua) University

The campus of Qinghua University lies about 10 kilometres from the urban districts. The Beijing Institute of Physical Culture lies to the north, the ruins of the Yuanmingyuan to the northwest, and Beijing University to the southwest. The Yiheyuan (Summer Palace) is only three kilometres away.

The Qinghua campus is tranquil and attractive. Its architecture is a mixture of traditional courtyard-style housing with painted beams and newer high-rise buildings. The oldest building on campus is an I-shaped structure, and over its main entrance hangs a sign with the characters "Qinghuayuan" (Park of Clear Splendour) inscribed in gold in the calligraphy of the Xianfeng emperor of the Qing dynasty. The entrance to Courtyard One, a classroom building completed early this century, bears the characters "Qinghua Xuetang" (Clear Splendour College) written by Natong, a Qing foreign minister,

Lu Xun (*third from left*) with Chinese and foreign friends at a meeting of the Esperanto Society in Beijing, May 23, 1922

Bedroom and workroom at Lu Xun's former residence inside Fu-chengmen, Beijing.

Translations made by Lu Xun.

Mamenxi dinosaur fossil, 22 metres long and 3.5 metres high, at the Beijing Museum of Natural History.

The over 500-years-old Beijing Observatory outside Jianguomen.

The new Beijing Library, the biggest in China, is situated to the north of the Purple Bamboo Park in Beijing's western suburbs.

The "stone library" of Confucian classics at the former Imperial College (the highest educational administration in the Ming and Qing dynasties), now the Capital Library.

Reading room.

Loan desk.

Book stacks.

Beijing University, one of the universities with the longest history in China.

Tombstone of Edgar Snow, an American friend of China, beside the Weiminghu (Unnamed Lake) at Beijing University; part of Snow's ashes are buried here.

Qinghua College, one of the earliest buildings at the Qinghua University.

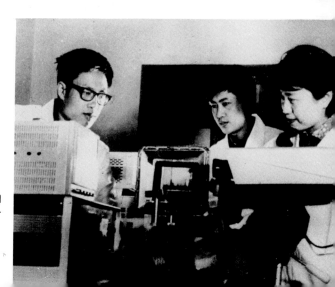

Students of optical instruments in laboratory.

Students in the Minority Languages and Literatures Department of the Central Institute for Nationalities listening to recordings.

An auditorium, library and gymnasium erected in the 1920s are placed like pieces on a chessboard amid older pavilions. The main classroom building and a stretch of new buildings were constructed after 1949. The overall impression is one of both age and modernity.

The Qinghuayuan was founded as an imperial park during the reign of the Kangxi emperor of the Qing dynasty. When the Daoguang emperor assumed the throne in 1821, he bestowed the Qinghuayuan on his fifth son, Yizong, who bequeathed it to his eldest son, Zailian. During the Boxer Uprising of 1900, the rebels set up garrisons in the park. Zailian was afterwards accused of aiding the Boxers and the park was confiscated by the Qing court.

In 1909, the United States returned part of the indemnities that China had paid in compensation for damages caused by the Boxers, agreeing that the sum was to be used to send Chinese students to the United States. The Qing foreign ministry decided to establish in some quiet and open space outside the capital a preparatory school for the students going to America. The Qinghuayuan was chosen as the site. The first school buildings there went up in 1911, and the school formally opened on April 29, 1911 and was named Qinghua College after the park. Its first batch of students was composed of 468 children aged 12 to 13 from 21 provinces. A university section was added in 1925 and the whole of Qinghua was formally transformed into a university in 1928. On the eve of the War Against Japan in 1937, Qinghua had become a general university with colleges of liberal arts, law, science and engineering. There were four main buildings, the auditorium, the library, the science hall and the gymnasium. The auditorium, which once held school-wide assemblies, now seats less than one-fifth of today's student body. The library behind the auditorium has expanded into one of the country's best-known collections, with a book stock totalling two million volumes, in Chinese and other languages. It holds nearly 2,000 technical journals in foreign languages, including the first issues of journals such as *Chemical Abstracts* (1907), *Physical Review* (1913) and *Metik und Mechanik* (1921). The library holds original bone and tortoise shell inscriptions from the Yin dynasty and local chronicles from around the country.

In 1952, Qinghua was reorganized into a polytechnical university. It now has 14 departments including hydraulic engineering, architectural engineering, civil and environmental engineering, mechanical engineering, chemistry and chemical engineering, physical engineering and economic management, and a nuclear energy research institute. From 1949 to 1965 more than 20,000 students graduated from Qinghua, over 20 times the number of graduates from the Qinghua Engineering College before Liberation. The university has played an important role in national scientific research and economic development. In the 1950s, Qinghua researchers developed the techniques of nodular cast iron, argon arc and electro-slag welding. In the 1960s, the university participated in research into programme-controlled machine tools, reactor shells for synthetic ammonia, the design and construction of a nuclear reactor and the construction of the Miyun Reservoir, the biggest in north China. And in the 1970s, Qinghua contributed to the study and manufacture of large-scale integrated circuits and phenylyclohexane liquid crystals.

The Qinghua campus gradually expanded eastward so that it now covers twice as great an area as before. Its floor space has increased from 100,000 square metres in 1949 to more than 500,000 square metres today.

Qinghua University was a democratic stronghold in pre-Liberation China even before nationwide democracy was achieved, and many Qinghua students were active in pre-Liberation patriotic student movements. It was Qinghua students who in 1935 issued the cry, "In the vastness of north China there is nowhere to study in peace and quiet," which triggered the nationwide December 9th Movement against Japanese aggression. Qinghua professors such as Wen Yiduo,[1] Zhu Ziqing[2] and Wu Han[3] took part in democratic movements in the mid and late 1940s.

The university has always been a meeting-place for eminent scholars and has nurtured many gifted professionals. Among the famous foreign scholars who have taught or lectured at the university in its early years are Norbert Wiener (1894-1964), founder of modern control theory, Theodor von Karman (1881-1963), founder of modern mechanics, and Frank Wattendorf, the great master of modern aeronautical theory and experiment; Chinese scholars have included Wang Guowei[4] (1877-1927), Liang Qichao[5] (1873-1929) and Zhao Yuanren.[6] Qinghua has produced many distinguished scientists and technicians as well as professionals in cultural and educational fields. Qinghua alumni include well-known mathematicians like Xiong Qinglai[7] and Hua Luogeng,[8] physicists like Qian Xuesen,[9] Qian Sanqiang[10] and Zhou Peiyuan,[11] chemists like Zhang Zigao,[12] archi-

[1]闻一多；[2]朱自清；[3]吴晗；[4]王国维；[5]梁启超；[6]赵元任；[7]熊庆来；[8]华罗庚；[9]钱学森；[10]钱三强；[11]周培源；[12]张子高。

tects like Liang Sicheng[1] and Yang Tingbao,[2] mecha-
nists like Qian Weichang[3] and Wu Zhonghua,[4] and some
of the best-known American scientists of Chinese origin
such as the Nobel Prize winners Tsung-dao Lee[5] (Li
Zhengdao) and Chen-ning Yang[6] (Yang Zhenning); C. C.
Lin[7] (Lin Jiaqiao); C. C. Chang[8] (Zhang Jieqian) and
C. K. Jen[9] (Ren Zhigong). Qinghua also educated a large
proportion of the researchers at the Academia Sinica
(Academy of Sciences of China): fifty-six pre-war graduates of Qinghua were appointed to the academy shortly after 1949, accounting for one-fifth of the total academic staff.

Some of the most prominent educators of this century in China have worked at Qinghua, including Professor Liu Xianzhou,[10] who was the university's vice-
chancellor for many years following Liberation. He has
worked in education for over 50 years, and engineers
and technicians throughout China have been trained
under him. Liu Xianzhou was the first Chinese scholar
to compile university textbooks in Chinese, and he has
also made a thorough study of the history of China's
ancient engineering inventions. Another illustrious
educator, Professor Liang Sicheng,[11] entered Qinghua as a student in 1915. Later he founded the
Department of Architecture at Qinghua and was its dean
for many years. After Liberation, he was named a member
of the Department of Technical Sciences under the Chinese
Academy of Sciences, Director of the Research Section for
Architectural History at the Chinese Academy of Architecture, and Deputy Chairman of the Beijing Municipal
Construction Committee. Liang also was a visiting pro-

[1]梁思成；[2]杨廷宝；[3]钱伟长；[4]吴仲华；[5]李政道；[6]杨振宁；[7]林
家翘；[8]张捷迁；[9]任之恭；[10]刘仙洲；[11]梁思成。

fessor at Yale University and a consultant to the design committee for the construction of the United Nations' headquarters building.

The university was an important centre for the development of modern drama in China. Between 1911 and 1921 the Qinghua Amateur Troupe staged over 100 plays; among its members were Hong Shen,[1] Li Jianwu[2] and Cao Yu[3] (Chia-pao Wan), who later formed the first generation of modern playwrights. Apart from plays such as *Lady Windermere's Fan* and *A Doll's House,* the troupe also performed Cao Yu's first play, *Leiyu*[4] (Thunderstorm) which was written at the library in his spare time.

Qinghua also numbers many well-known social activists among its graduates, such as Ji Chaoding,[5] late Chairman of the China Association for the Promotion of International Trade; Yao Yilin,[6] Chairman of the State Planning Commission; Jiang Nanxiang,[7] Minister of Education, Li Chang,[8] Deputy President of the Chinese Academy of Sciences, and Yu Guangyuan,[9] leading economist in China and Deputy President of the Chinese Academy of Social Sciences.

Qinghua has long been an important centre of international academic and friendly exchange. In the 1930s, the school signed agreements with institutions, including the German Far East Association, the International Cultural Exchange Office and the Franco-Chinese Cultural Fund, for the exchange of postgraduate students and provision of facilities for scientific research. Qinghua also exchanged postgraduates with the Association of German Universities in 1935. At that time, many

[1]洪深；[2]李健吾；[3]曹禺；[4]《雷雨》；[5]冀朝鼎；[6]姚依林；[7]蒋南翔；[8]李昌；[9]于光远。

Qinghua professors on vacation abroad were invited to lecture at Western universities as visiting scholars. This practice came to an end during the War of Resistance Against Japan. Since Liberation, scientists like Tsung-dao Lee, Chen-ning Yang, and C. C. Lin have frequently lectured at Qinghua while faculty members from Qinghua such as Liu Xianzhou, Zhang Wei[1] and Zhang Guang-dou[2] have travelled abroad to research and lecture. Through the years, many foreign students have come to study at Qinghua, and Qinghua has sent teachers and students abroad to study. Several thousand alumni took part in the 70th anniversary of the founding of Qinghua University in April, 1981.

The Central Institute for Nationalities

As a country of many nationalities, China attaches great importance to the training of minority nationality leaders and specialists. More than ten institutes have been set up specifically for this purpose since 1949, including the Central Institute for Nationalities in Beijing.

The institute is located along the road to the Yihe-yuan (Summer Palace), not far from the Capital Stadium where international sports events are held. Inside the compound gates are a dozen buildings in different national styles, including classrooms, an auditorium, a library and dormitories. Signs and notices in minority scripts and students dressed in their national costumes lend a special air to the campus.

Apart from training minority personnel, the institute also conducts historical, cultural, social and econom-

[1]张维；[2]张光斗。

ic research on each of China's 56 nationalities. The school had 200 students when it first opened, and now has 2,600 students of different nationalities.

In the past, many of China's minority nationalities suffered from oppression and poverty, and those with small populations in border areas were on the verge of extinction. Schooling in minority regions was unheard of. Today, minority young people come to study in Beijing each year in increasing numbers. At the institute, they get free lodging, board and medical care, and those holding their former appointments continue to receive their pay.

The institute has six departments (politics, minority languages and literature, Han language and literature, arts, history, mathematics and physics), a cadres' training course and a preparatory school.

Departmental students are enrolled through the nation's university entrance exams. Undergraduate study lasts four years, and the government makes work assignments for every graduate. The cadres' training course enrolls cadres above county or commune level from the minority regions. The 12 to 18 month course concentrates on political theory and current policies, as well as general knowledge.

The Minority Languages and Literature Department turns out linguists and translators. It covers more than a dozen minority languages, including Mongolian, Korean, Tibetan, Uygur, Kazak, Yi, Turkic and ancient Tibetan. Apart from minority students who come to study their own languages and literature, the department also enrolls Han students. Classes are conducted in minority languages. The majority of the teaching staff are from among the minorities, and the Han teachers also know minority languages.

The Arts Department offers courses in music, dance and fine arts. Most of China's minority nationalities have their own styles of singing and dancing, and on festival days the students demonstrate their skills. Strict professional training is given, and students also take part in the activities of uncovering and reassessing their cultural heritage.

The institute also has a research department, which is devoted to the study of theoretical problems and policies related to nationalities, history, languages, literature and art. It is staffed by more than 100 researchers, who make frequent trips to minority areas to carry out investigations and write reports, theses and contributions to the academic study of national minorities. The Archeological Office collects, studies and exhibits historical relics of minorities. Its collection now numbers over 30,000 items, ranging from drums and bowls made of human skin and skulls, evidence of the cruelty of Tibetan serf-owners, to the stone pots of the Dulong nationality and the record-keeping bamboo strips of the Va nationality. There are weapons used by minorities in uprisings since the time of the Ming dynasty, such as the broad swords used in the uprising of 1572 by the Miao, Zhuang, Dong and Yao nationalities from the Great Miao Mountain in Guangxi. There is a rich collection of tools, religious objects and articles of daily use, and also clothing and personal adornments exhibiting a high level of design and craftsmanship, with several hundred examples of Miao embroidered belts and aprons alone.

On the west side of the campus is a small building housing the institute library. Of the library's 700,000 volumes, more than 80,000 are in over 20 minority national languages, such as Mongolian, Tibetan, Uygur, Zhuang, Buyi, Korean, Manchu, Jingpo, Xibo, Kirgiz and Naxi. There are materials in the Huigu script of the Uygur, the ancient script of the Dai nationality, the pictographic script of the Naxi nationality, rubbings of ancient tablet inscriptions in ancient Qidan and Nüzhen (Jurchen) script and examples of ancient Xixia script. Also in the collection are a history of Tibet written in ancient Tibetan during the Qing dynasty *Life of Puoluona,* a Buddhist sutra in the Dai language inscribed on palm leaves, and a bilingual edition of the novel *Jinpingmei* in Manchu and Han. The library has more than 2,500 volumes of local chronicles, many from areas with minority nationalities such as Tibet, Xinjiang, Inner Mongolia and Yunnan. The library has seven reading rooms, including one furnished with journals in 28 languages from various minority nationality areas.

Full attention is paid to the languages of the nationalities at the institute. The staff and students speak freely in their own languages, and notices are posted in minority languages.

Traditional minority festivals like the Islamic *Qurban,* the Tibetan New Year and the Torch Festival of the Yi nationality are fully observed with the appropriate celebrations. To cater for different dietary customs Moslem canteens have been set up for Islamic students from more than ten nationalities including the Hui, Uygur, Kazak, Kirgiz, Ozbek, Sala; other canteens serve national dishes such as *zhuafan* (spicy mutton rice eaten with fingers) and *kaonang* (a kind of sweet cake) from Xinjiang, butter tea from Tibet and milk tea from pastoral area.

Since its founding in 1951, the institute has turned out more than 15,000 graduates from over 50 nationalities. Most have returned to their homes where they have made great contributions. Some are already in leading positions, such as Pudoje, Vice-Chairman of the Tibet Autonomous Regional Government, and Tomur Dawamat, Chairman of the Standing Committee of the People's Congress in Xinjiang Uygur Autonomous Region. Other graduates include the Tibetan mountaineers Kombu and Paindog, members of the first group of climbers to reach the peak of Mount Jolmolungma from the north slope, and quite a number of associate professors teaching in this institute. Because of its special nature, the institute attracts several thousand visitors from foreign countries every year.

12

Beijing Arts and Crafts

The cultural life of Beijing is rich in a variety of arts and crafts famous not only in China but across the world. In this chapter some of these are described, including Beijing Opera, wood-block colour printing, jade and ivory carving, cloisonne and carpets.

Beijing Opera

Beijing Opera was originally a form of local theatre in north China, but its popularity has now spread all over the country. Like most Chinese local operas, it is truly a comprehensive art combining stylized acting with singing, acrobatics and colourful costumes. It has become the most popular and influential of over a hundred kinds of dramatic forms on the Chinese stage.

Beijing Opera dates back more than 150 years to the time of the Qianlong emperor of the Qing dynasty. On his frequent hunting expeditions in south-central China, Qianlong developed an interest in the local operas. In 1790, to celebrate his eightieth birthday, he summoned opera troupes from different localities to perform for him in Beijing. Four famous troupes from Anhui Province remained in Beijing after the celebrations, and the vigorous clear tunes of Anhui Opera gradually replaced Kunqu Opera, which had been popular in the palace and among the upper classes in Beijing. In 1828, a Hubei troupe came to Beijing and often performed together with the Anhui troupes. The two types of singing blended on the same stage and gradually gave birth to a new genre which came to be known as Beijing Opera. Beijing Opera therefore has incorporated the best elements from operatic forms.

The singing in Beijing Opera is highly stylized but its variations of rhythm and pitch enable the performer to express the thoughts and emotions of different characters in different situations. Recitatives may be in dialogue and monologue form; either a special kind of musical speech, *yunbai* (rhythmic vernacular), or standard spoken Chinese, *jingbai* (capital vernacular), may be employed. Acting in Beijing Opera encompasses a set range of movements, gestures and expressions. Every movement or pose, such as stroking a beard, setting a hat straight, swinging a sleeve or lifting a foot, has its own "formula" or pattern which has been reduced to its essentials and perfected.

The art of illusion is one of Beijing Opera's most important characteristics, expressed through techniques of exaggeration and concentration. It can be said Beijing Opera performers conquer time and space. Backdrops and stage props are kept to a minimum; often a table and two chairs in front of a big curtain is regarded as sufficient. The three dimensional stage props of modern Western drama is seen as superfluous or even as an encumbrance. The performers use gestures and body movements to represent actions such as opening and closing a door, going up or down a building or a mountain, and

embarking, disembarking or travelling by boat. A decorated whip represents a horse, a paddle a boat and
two pennants embroidered with wheels a carriage. When
an actor walks in a circle, it means he has gone on a long
journey. Four generals and four soldiers signifies an
army thousands strong. Two actors can portray grop-
ing and fighting in the dark through dance and acrobatics on a brightly lit stage. By such techniques, passed
down and developed by generations of performers, Beijing Opera has made it possible to transform a small
stage into the whole universe.

Stringed and wind instruments are used for the
musical accompaniment to Beijing Opera, but even more
characteristic are the percussion instruments — gongs and
drums of different sizes and types, and castanets made of
padauk wood and bamboo. The most important stringed
instrument is the *jinghu* (a kind of two-stringed fiddle)
followed by the *erhu* (also a two-stringed fiddle), plus
some plucked instruments such as *yueqin* (a kind of man-
dolin with four strings). The stringed instruments are played in unison but do not practise Western-style harmony.

The character roles in Beijing Opera are finely dif-
ferentiated according to age and disposition. Female
roles are called *dan*, male roles are *sheng*, clowns are
chou. Roles characterized by the use of different patterns of facial make-up which distinguish a rough, frank
character from a cruel or sinister one are called *jing jiao*
or *hua lian* (painted faces); the audience knows from
the colours and patterns what kind of character is being
portrayed. For instance, red signifies loyalty and courage, yellow signifies fierceness, white usually signifies
villainy and black signifies honesty and straightfor-
wardness. Spirits, monsters, immortals and Buddhas are

often identified by gold and silver. There are different performing styles also for each of these role types, including different styles of singing.

The elaborate and gorgeous costuming of Beijing Opera is one of its special characteristics. They are based on the style of Ming dynasty costume, with much use of deep red, deep green, yellow, white, black and blue. Strongly contrasting colours are freely used, and embroidery in gold, silver and coloured thread. There are strict rules for costumes based on rank character and life-style. The stage props are decorated and beautified versions of their real-life counterparts, and are often works of art in themselves.

The plot-development of Beijing Opera does not conform to the general pattern of other types of drama. In the modern theatre and cinema, the struggle between heroes and villains is gradually developed, and the final outcome is left to the end. In Beijing Opera, the heroes and villains revealed as soon as they come on stage. The audience for Beijing Opera have gone beyond the desire to know the outcome: they are already familiar with the plots about the Monkey King, Xiang Yu the Conqueror, the women generals of the Yang family. It is rather the magic of the performance itself and the skilful techniques of the singing, dancing and acrobatics which attract them. For this reason the same piece can be seen over and over again without boredom. The first performer to introduce Beijing Opera abroad was the famous *dan* actor Mei Lanfang,[1] who went to Japan in 1919, to the United States in 1929 and to the Soviet Union in 1935. In 1932, another famous Beijing Opera performer, Cheng Yanqiu,[2] made a

[1]梅兰芳；[2]程砚秋。

tour of Europe and gave performances and lectures. Since Liberation, Beijing Opera troupes have made frequent trips abroad, to places such as Japan, Europe, Latin America, the United States and Africa. Today Beijing Opera has won high praise around the world.

Watercolour Wood-Block Printing

Rongbaozhai, Studio of Glorious Treasures, is a world-renowned art shop in Beijing. Its fame comes from its watercolour wood-block printing, used to make fine reproductions of paintings and calligraphy. It was founded more than 200 years ago in the period of transition between Qing emperors Qianlong and Jiajing as an undertaking of the Qing imperial family. Originally known as Songzhuzhai (Pine and Bamboo Studio) it acquired its present name in 1894.

Before Liberation, Rongbaozhai merely printed and sold illustrated letter-sized notepaper. Since 1949, however, the shop with government support has become a flourishing business enterprise with the capacity to reproduce masterpieces of painting and calligraphy. It also offers for sale original paintings and calligraphy scrolls, bronze and stone rubbings, and the "four treasures of the study" (writing brushes, ink slabs, ink sticks and paper). It has become a cultural centre where well-known Chinese painters and calligraphers demonstrate their skills.

Watercolour wood-block printing is a special printing method developed to suit the characteristics of Chinese painting. The Rongbaozhai reproductions made by this technique are extraordinarily true to the original. The secret is in using the same materials as the original to duplicate its subject and style. This of course requires an extremely high degree of skill and experience.

The first step in the reproduction is to trace the original with Chinese ink on transparent paper, making one copy for each colour in the original. These tracings are then pasted on wood-blocks to guide the carvers. When a block has been carved for each colour, impressions are made one by one to form the reproduction, using the same paper, ink and pigments as in the original work. Because the inks and paints used in Chinese paintings are water-based rather than oil-based, the whole process is called watercolour wood-block printing. Reproductions made by this method look so authentic that even if they are hanging side by side with the original a layman can hardly distinguish the original from the copy.

Watercolour wood-block printing goes back more than 1,000 years in China. The earliest sample of this technique is a simple one-colour portrait of Buddha made in 868, found in one of the famous Dunhuang Grottoes in Gansu.

Rongbaozhai began to reproduce the works of famous Chinese painters in the early 1950s. By the 1960s, it was able to reproduce the thousand-year-old scroll *The Night Entertainment of Han Xizai* by Gu Hongzhong,[1] a painting which depicts the life of the ancient nobility. Because of its age and the complexity of its composition and colour scheme, it took eight years to reproduce and required 1,660 separate wood blocks. The studio has also scored great successes in reproducing later works such as Zhou Fang's[2] *Ladies with Flower Headdress* from the Tang dynasty, Ma Yuan's[3] *Singing While Strolling* from the Song, Wen Zhengming's[4] *Orchid*

[1]顾闳中；[2]周昉；[3]马远；[4]文征明。

Pavilion Purification Ceremony from the Ming, Zheng Banqiao's[1] *Orchid and Bamboo* and Wu Changshuo's[2] *Peaches,* both from the Qing. Among the many works by modern painters it has reproduced, the most popular include Xu Beihong's[3] *Spring Rain on Lijiang River* and *Fish Hawks,* He Xiangning's[4] *Plum Blossoms,* Qi Baishi's[5] *Free-hand Flowers* and Wu Zuoren's[6] *Pandas.* The studio is now working on two famous old paintings, *The Qingming Festival on the River* by Zhang Zeduan[7] of the Song and *Guo Ladies Touring in Spring* by Zhang Xuan[8] of the Tang, both from the Palace Museum collection in Beijing. Reproductions of paintings by Qi Baishi, Xu Beihong, Huang Binhong,[9] Fu Baoshi[10] and Pan Tianshou[11] are always in stock, and even their originals are on sale from time to time.

Watercolour wood-block printing is such meticulous work that even simple paintings like a galloping horse in black ink by Xu Beihong or several chickens by Qi Baishi require dozens of wood blocks and scores of impressions. The studio's craftsmen pay serious attention to the work of training their successors. Tian Yongqing,[12] a veteran craftsman who has been with the studio for nearly fifty years, has been training apprentices since shortly after Liberation. Now more than 60 middle-aged and younger craftsmen have learned the trade under his supervision.

Today the walls of Rongbaozhai's spacious showroom at Liulichang in the southern part of Beijing feature a superb collection of original works and reproductions of painting and calligraphy. There are land-

---

[1]郑板桥；[2]吴昌硕；[3]徐悲鸿；[4]何香凝；[5]齐白石；[6]吴作人；[7]张择端；[8]张萱；[9]黄宾虹；[10]傅抱石；[11]潘天寿；[12]田永庆。

scapes, portraits, paintings of flowers, birds, plants and insects, some on scrolls and some on fans.   There are counters selling rice paper from Jingxian in Anhui, painting brushes made in Beijing by Li Fushou, pigments made in Suzhou by Jiang Sixu, and ink-slabs made in Keshan in Zhaoqingfu, Guangdong. Also on sale are rubbings, printed albums and writing paper. The art shop attracts large numbers of Chinese and foreign customers. In 1978, about 80,000 people paid visits here.   In recent years, reproductions from the studio have come to be sold in more than 50 countries and regions and buyers from more than a dozen countries make direct purchases. A Rongbaozhai exhibition in Tokyo in 1979 attracted large crowds.

Handicrafts

Beijing has long been known for the wide variety and exquisite workmanship of its handicrafts.   The foreign market for them dates back to the first two decades of this century, when many Beijing handicrafts including jade and ivory carvings, cloisonne, carved lacquerware, filigree, carpets, lanterns and porcelain won gold prizes at the Panamanian International Fairs and high praise at other fairs held in London, Nagoya and elsewhere.

Other handicrafts include flowers made of satin or silk; animals, birds and flowers made of coloured glass; figurines of painted clay; and head ornaments of velvet flowers and birds worn on festival days. Beijing handicrafts have developed greatly since 1949, and more than 40 crafts are now being practised.

Jade Carving

Jade carving has a long history in China. As early as the Shang and Zhou dynasties it had become a separate profession and excavations have shown the fine workmanship of that time. Jade is the general name given to a fine hard stone, either jadeite or nephrite. The colour is usually white or green. Other precious stones are also used in carving, such as red agate, white agate, crystal, amethyst, jadeite, coral, ruby and sapphire, and these are often also loosely referred to as "jade".

A piece of finely carved jade made of high-quality stone can be worth a great deal of money. For example, a pair of green jadeite pendants of a dragon and a phoenix made in the spring of 1978 by the Beijing Jadeware Workshop fetched RMB 1,800,000 yuan in Hongkong. The relief carvings of a dragon, a phoenix, two butterflies and the Chinese *shuangxi* (double happiness) character on pendants smaller than matchboxes achieve an effect of great depth. Other examples are carvings of a Buddha with many arms, dragons or a parrot resting on a ring carved out of a piece of coral.

The craftsmen of the Beijing Jadeware Workshop are particularly skilled in exploiting the natural colour of a piece of jade to create an effective design. A jadeite *Vase with Three Reminders of Autumn*, for example, has dark green katydids resting on cucumber leaves and green cucumbers and vines twining around the pale blue vase. *Stealing the Fairyland Herb*, a white jade statuette based on a Chinese folktale, depicts a fair maiden clad in white with red trimmings, with a black *lingzhi* in her mouth, in flight from her pursuers. Both these articles manifest the craftsmen's ingenuity in utilizing natural colouration in their creations.

Beijing jadeware such as vases, incense burners, incense stands and tripods are generally severe and well-proportioned, with simple, classical decorations; some, however, are more elaborately decorated with gold and silver filigree and precious stones. Jade flower carving is a different kind of product, including such objects as jade flower baskets, flower vases, miniature trees and rock gardens, and individual flowers such as plum-blossom, orchids, chrysanthemums, Chinese roses and peonies. Fret-work and relief carving produce very life-like objects. Birds and animals, depicted flying, eating or at rest, form another category of Beijing jadeware. Still another category includes rings, bead-necklaces, earrings, pendants, seals and cigarette holders.

Ivory Carving

Ivory carving in China was already fairly well developed as early as the Warring States Period some 2,000 years ago, but in Beijing it did not become well-established until the Ming dynasty. By the Qing dynasty this craft had reached a high level of artistry, and works of that time are now preserved in the Palace Museum. Since 1949, Beijing ivory carving has further developed its techniques and extended its themes to contemporary life.

Figure carving is a popular theme. Even at the present time, Chinese history, legend and romantic fiction provide the inspiration for many creations, especially beautiful women. Flower carving is also very popular. The "Grain of Rice" is a famous type of Beijing ivory carving. To the naked eye there is only a grain of rice, but under a ten-power magnifier, the grain is seen to be a piece of ivory with an engraving of a classical poem in exquisite Chinese calligraphy, a landscape or some historical scene. A building will be complete with carved beams and painted rafters, and landscape or scene from an ancient story will be peopled with miniscule figures.

Cloisonne

Cloisonne is a handicraft in which coloured enamels are applied to designs outlined in copper wire on a bronze object. The craft first appeared in the Yuan dynasty and developed greatly during the Jingtai reign of the Ming. "Jingtai Blue" is the name of the dazzling colour of one of the most frequently used cloisonne enamels introduced at that time, and is now used to refer to cloisonne enamels in general.

The cloisonne process begins with the casting of bronze into different shapes — vases, bowls and the like — to which flat bronze wires are then affixed in decorative patterns. Enamels of different colours are applied to fill the *cloisons* or hollows. Each cloisonne piece is fired three times with a fresh coat of enamel each time. After firing, the pieces are ground and polished, and look to be gilded.

Techniques of wire filigree in cloisonne production were very sophisticated by the time of Qianlong in the Qing dynasty, and a variety of patterns of great subtlety and grace were used. Chinese cloisonne was introduced to the world market in the last years of the Qing dynasty, and in 1904 it received a first prize at the Chicago World Fair.

Since 1949, cloisonne craftsmanship has undergone great development in two respects. First, the colour range of enamels has been extended to pea green, rose

purple, coffee, egg yellow, azure and gold. Most cloisonne pieces made now are polychrome, and are polished
to create various tones. Secondly, the designs have been
improved by borrowing from patterns found on old silks.

Over the past few years, cloisonne production has
begun to shift away from the purely decorative and towards items for practical use, such as dinner sets, tea
sets, wine sets, lamps and lanterns. The most recent
products are case and wall ornaments.

Lacquerware

Chinese lacquerware originated in the Han dynasty.
It reached Beijing during the Tang dynasty, more than
1,000 years ago, and techniques improved steadily
through the Yuan and Ming dynasties.

Beijing lacquerware starts with a copper body lined
inside with enamel and with a gilded rim; lacquerware
with wooden body or from a clay cast is also very common.
A hundred coats of lacquer are then applied to the outside, or in some cases three hundred or even five hundred layers, to a thickness of 5-18 mm. After the lacquer
has dried, it is carved with landscapes, figures, flowers,
birds, animals or other patterns. More than thirty different kinds of goods were traditionally produced, including everyday items such as vases, plates, boxes and
jars, and decorative objects such as screens. In the past,
they were made in only four colours, but the number of
colours has increased to over 20 today. Older pieces
are invariably monochrome, but polychrome pieces are
now being produced. Nevertheless, the traditional dark
red monochrome ware is still the most common.

Carving techniques include relief and fretwork.
The carving is delicate and precise, and often achieves

a three-dimensional effect. Lacquerware is prized for its lasting qualities, the result of the painstaking procedures used in its creation.

Carpets

Carpet-making goes back at least 2,000 years in China. It reached Beijing only in the Xianfeng and Tongzhi reigns of the Qing dynasty, when Tibetan lamas were summoned to the capital to set up a carpet training shop at the Baoguosi to produce carpets for the imperial palaces. The carpets were made of closely woven fine woollen yarn. Many different patterns were employed. Some had a dragon and a phoenix at the centre, or the Chinese character *shou*, meaning longevity; around the borders were symmetrical designs of peonies, plum blossoms, pine branches, citrons, peaches, lions, goats, cranes and bats; and wheels, conch shells, parasols, lutes, chess pieces and paintings embellished the empty spaces. By the end of the Qing dynasty, Beijing carpets had gained fame both at home and abroad, and were awarded a first prize at the World Fair of 1903.

Most of today's Beijing carpets have traditional flower patterns. Other popular designs based on traditional motifs include lions rolling with balls, two dragons playing with a pearl, or five bats surrounding the Chinese character *shou*. These carpets are famous for their bright colours, softness and durability.

13

Beijing Cuisine

Chinese cuisine is famed the world over for its appearance, aroma and flavour. Its unique style of preparation, cooking and presentation dates back to the beginnings of Chinese history in remote antiquity. As the capital of China for many centuries, Beijing developed its own cuisine combining the best features of different regional styles. Beijing cuisine reached its present form in the imperial kitchens of the Qing dynasty. Among the most well-known dishes or styles which found their way from the court to public restaurants are Beijing Roast Duck, Court Cuisine, Tan Cuisine, Rinsed Mutton and Barbecued Meat.

Beijing Roast Duck

Beijing Roast Duck dates back some 600 years to the Ming dynasty. Apart from the two Beijing restaurants which specialize in this dish, many other major restaurants also serve it now.

The earliest Beijing Roast Duck restaurant is the Bianyifang (Shop of Convenience and Pleasure), founded more than four hundred years ago, in Rice Market *hutong* in the old Vegetable Market area in the

southern city.   This place had closed down by 1949, but
another Bianyifang was opened in 1855 just beyond Qianmen and is still in operation. The most famous Beijing
Roast Duck restaurant is the Quanjude (Complete Collection of Virtues), opened in 1864, also outside Qianmen.
The founder of the Quanjude was Yang Quanren.   It is
said that he came to Beijing from nearby Jixian in 1835
and started up a duck and chicken stall (consisting of a
plank across two stools) in the Meat Market outside Qianmen. In time, the stall became a shop and within a decade,
the proprietor had made enough money to convert the
shop into a restaurant specializing in Beijing Roast
Duck. By the time Yang's son inherited the family business, the Quanjude was recognized throughout China
as the leading Beijing Roast Duck restaurant.

       After 1949, the Quanjude and Bianyifang became
joint state-private enterprises. Later, as business developed, each opened up three branches. The newest is
the seven-story Beijing Roast Duck Restaurant, a branch
of the Quanjude, which opened in 1979 near Hepingmen
(Peace Gate) in the southwest part of the city. With a
floor space of 15,000 square metres divided into 41 dining rooms of different sizes, it can serve 3,000 customers
simultaneously.   Each floor with dining rooms has its
own kitchen, and with all kitchens working at maximum
capacity 1,000 ducks a day can be served.

       Beijing Roast Duck has two distinctive characteris-
tics, the superior quality of the duck itself and its
unique style of preparation.

       The duck is a specially-bred and fatted variety,
raised on the dozen or so poultry farms dotted around
the city where the water is of good quality and pond
plant life is abundant. The duck is usually ready when

it is 65 days old and weighs 2 kilogrammes. For its last three weeks, it is force-fed four times a day with a rich mixture of millet, mung beans, sorghum and wheat chaff and not allowed to move freely. The duck is thus bred for roasting, with plenty of meat on the breast, a thin skin and tender flesh.

After the duck is killed, plucked and cleaned, compressed air is injected between the skin and the flesh to produce a plump, firm-looking bird. The skin is then scalded with boiling water, so that the pores contract and the albumin in the skin congeals, the air under the skin expands and inflates the skin, and the skin becomes glossy and shiny. The next step is to coat the skin with syrup, which gives the duck a rich, red colour and makes the skin crisp when it is roasted. The duck is then hung in a cool, shady, well-ventilated place to dry.

The duck is now ready to cook. First, a precise amount of boiling water is poured in through the rump and the opening is plugged. When the duck is put into the oven, the water is converted into steam, cooking the duck meat from inside while the skin is being browned. In this way, the skin is crisp and the flesh remains tender.

The method of roasting Beijing Duck goes back several hundred years, and many different variations exist. The most common way is to use a specially designed wall oven with parallel horizontal bars from which the ducks dangle while cooking. Hardwood fuel (usually jujube, peach or pear wood, which produce the least smoke) is burned in a fire-pit in front of the oven. The heat from the pit is reflected to the roof of the oven then to the suspended ducks.   The reflected heat cooks the ducks evenly, and the fuel imparts a special aroma.

The Bianyifang uses a slightly different method inherited from the original restaurant of that name.   Instead of using an open fire outside, the oven is preheated by burning millet stalks inside; then the ducks are hung inside and the oven door is closed, so that the ducks are browned by the heat radiating from the oven walls.

Correct temperature control is vital.   The oven is heated to 250°C and the ducks inside should be turned regularly.   After 30-40 minutes, when the duck becomes an evenly deep red colour, it is ready to satisfy the visual, olfactory and gustatory demands of the most fastidious gourmet.

Beijing Roast Duck is also served in a unique way. Usually it is sliced into 120 thin pieces within 5-6 minutes after it is taken from the oven.   Each piece includes both skin and meat.   The slices are then wrapped by each diner in a thin pancake or stuffed into a hollow sesame seed bun with shredded green onions and minced garlic in a sweet bean sauce, and with thinly sliced cucumber or turnip in season.   People with a sweet tooth sometimes eat the duck with sugar.

More than 100 different hot and cold dishes can be prepared from the wings, webs, tongue, heart and liver. Eaten as preliminary to the main dish, they compose a "Complete Duck Banquet".

Beijing Roast Duck has an international reputation for excellence.   Many countries have requested Chinese assistance in establishing Beijing Roast Duck restaurants, and a Tokyo Branch of the Quanjude was formally opened in 1980.

Court Cuisine

Court Cuisine, as the name suggests, consists of dishes once prepared for the imperial family. Every dynasty in Chinese history had an "imperial kitchen" to prepare meals for the emperor and his consorts. The dishes were not only meticulously prepared, but also included rare and expensive foodstuffs such as bears' paws, birds' nests, sharks' fins, venison, sea slugs, duck webs and other delicacies of land and sea. The Court Cuisine of today is based on the dishes prepared by the Qing imperial kitchens.

There are two restaurants in Beijing where it is available: the Fangshan Restaurant in the Beihai Park, the former Winter Palace of the Qing emperors, and the Tingliguan Restaurant in the Yiheyuan, the former Summer Palace.

Fangshan (Imperial-Style) Restaurant occupies a splendid building in a fine location on Qionghuadao, with the lake in front and the hill behind. The restaurant has eleven dining rooms, large and small, with names like the Hall of Rippling Waves, the Studio of Tranquillity and the Tower of Azure Light. Its dishes are carefully prepared and beautifully served; the taste is subtle and clear, the textures crisp and tender. Take the "goldfish duck webs" for instance: the main ingredient is duck webs, to which are added mandarin fish, egg white, bacon, peas, wine and vegetable garnishes, the whole arranged in the shape of a goldfish.

The Fangshan Restaurant is also well-known for its delicate pastries, including pea flour cakes, kidney bean flour rolls, miniature corn cakes and sesame seed buns with chopped meat filling. These pastries originated among the ordinary people of Beijing and there are interesting stories about how they were introduced to the Qing court. For example, corn cakes found their way into the court in 1900 when the allied forces of the eight powers occupied Beijing. On her flight to Xi'an, several thousand kilometres away, the Empress Dowager Cixi was so hungry that she ate a corn cake, a staple food of poor families in north China. She liked the taste so much that upon her return to Beijing she ordered the imperial kitchen to make corn cakes for her. But the cooks, afraid that ordinary corn cakes might be too rough for the aged Cixi to eat, made miniature cakes with finely-ground corn flour and white sugar instead.

The Tingliguan (Hall for Listening to the Orioles) was a theatre in the Summer Palace where the Empress Dowager used to enjoy opera and music; the name implies that the imperial music was as beautiful as the singing of orioles. After 1949, it was converted into a restaurant. It is divided into eight dining rooms of various sizes in two courtyards, and can serve 500 customers at one time.

The menu is based on the Imperial Cuisine, and the experienced chefs can prepare more than 300 dishes and pastries from Qing and Ming imperial recipes. Crisp spiced chicken, a favourite of the Qianlong emperor, is made from tender young pullets, each weighing about one kilogramme. The pullets are steamed with Shaoxing rice wine, sugar, shredded green onions, ginger, sesame oil, peanut oil and five-spice powder (compounded of anise, cinnamon, Sichuan pepper, Chinese prickly ash and dried orange peel), allowed to cool and dry, and then fried until golden brown. The skin is then crisp, the flesh tender and the aroma and taste are delicious.

A new service provided by the restaurant is an all-fish banquet, using fresh fish from the Kunming Lake in more than 50 cold and hot dishes, soups and pastries. One famous dish is called "eating live Kunming Lake carp". The diners catch the fish themselves with nets from a fish tank. The scaling, splitting, cleaning, frying and garnishing takes two chefs working together less than four minutes. When the fish comes to the table, its mouth is still opening and closing and its gills flapping, and this can last for 20 to 30 minutes. The mouth sometimes keeps going even when the fish has been eaten down to the bones. The secret lies in keeping the nerve centre of the fish intact, which only chefs of superb skill and swiftness can do.

Tan Cuisine

Tan Cuisine is one of four cooking styles (the other three are Sichuan, Guangdong and Huai) offered at the Beijing Hotel. It originated in the household of Tan Zongjun,[1] a bureaucrat of late Qing times. Very particular about their food and drink, Tan Zongjun and his son Tan Zhuanqing[2] would pay high fees to hire skilled chefs to cook at their home, and then fire them after learning all their techniques. In this way the Tan family created a cuisine based on Guangdong cuisine and incorporating the best elements of other regional styles. The private dinner parties given at the Tan house gradually made their cuisine famous. After the fall of the Qing dynasty, the now impoverished Tans opened a small restaurant, and thus the Tan dishes found their way into

[1]谭宗浚；[2]谭篆青。

society, becoming a Beijing speciality of home-style cooking.

Tan Cuisine has three main features. First, it is both sweet and salty, balancing northern and southern styles. There is a saying that "southerners have a sweet tooth, and northerners crave salt", but Tan dishes manage to satisfy both. Secondly, the dishes are well-cooked, well-flavoured and soft, and so are considered suitable for older people. Thirdly, this type of cooking pays special attention to the natural flavours of the ingredients, so gourmet powder and other such seasonings are rarely used.

After Liberation, the Tan family formally opened a restaurant named Enchengju on Xidan Street. In 1954, it became a state-run enterprise and in 1958 it was moved to Beijing Hotel. The master chef is Peng Changhai,[1] who began to help in the Tan kitchen at the age of 17, and is thoroughly familiar with the Tan style. Steamed chicken with mushrooms and duck with crab meat are among his most popular dishes.

Rinsed Mutton

Rinsed Mutton (also known as mutton hot-pot) is a Hui (Muslim) speciality. In winter, the family and friends would gather round the fire and eat in intimacy and warmth. It has now spread to people of all nationalities in Beijing and become one of the capital's most celebrated dishes. The "hot-pot" is a brass pot with a wide outer rim around a chimney and a charcoal-burner underneath. Water is heated to boiling point in the rim, and the diners dip thin slices of raw mutton into the

[1]彭长海。

water, where the meat cooks rapidly. The cooked slices are then dipped into a sauce.

The sauce is individually mixed by each diner from an array of more than a dozen condiments such as sesame paste, Shaoxing rice wine, fermented bean curd, salted Chinese chive-flowers, soy sauce, chili paste, shrimp paste, rice vinegar, chopped green onion and minced coriander. Only raw meat, vegetables and seasonings are provided, and the diners cook and serve themselves. This makes for a rather active meal.

Rinsed Mutton has a history of over a thousand years, when chicken, fish and pork were also cooked in hot-pots. In the mid-seventeenth century, Rinsed Mutton was part of the winter menu at the Qing court. The first restaurant to serve Rinsed Mutton in Beijing was the Zhengyanglou Restaurant, which opened for business in 1855 (the same year as the Bianyifang). It closed down in 1942.

Today, Rinsed Mutton is available in almost all Hui restaurants in Beijing. The most famous is Donglaishun on Wangfujing Street, a Muslim restaurant which opened in 1903. Its techniques of slicing and seasoning were based on the Zhengyanglou, but with further improvements. The meat is extraordinarily tender, tasty and not at all rank.

Beijing Rinsed Mutton is famous for three things: choice cuts of mutton, wafer-thin slices, and skilful seasoning. The Donglaishun Restaurant uses only wethers weighing about 25 kilogrammes raised in the East and West Wuzhumuqin Banners (minority areas) in the Inner Mongolian Autonomous Region in northern China. The meat is white and tender and does not have the rank smell of meat from older sheep. Only the loin and legs

Dragon Gate on a Spring Morning (ivory carving).

Peacock Pot (cloisonne).

"Phoenix Nest", made of a whole chicken and quail eggs, from the Court Cuisine.

Beijing Roast Duck.

Pea Flour Cakes, Kidney Bean
Rolls, Corn-Flour Cakes, and
Thousand-Layer Cakes, from the
Court Cuisine.

A scene from the Beijing Opera *Story of a White Snake*, a folk legend.

Cunning and trickery.

Honesty and probity.

Courage and ferocity.

Impartiality and fortitude.

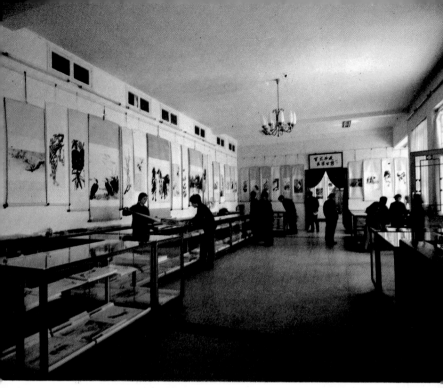

Interior of Rongbaozhai, famous for its reproductions
of Chinese calligraphy and painting.

are used, about 8 kilogrammes per animal. Meat scraps, gristle and sinews are trimmed off, and the remaining meat is cut into thin slices about 4 cm long and 2 cm wide. Each slice has both fat and lean meat and is so thin as to be translucent.

Barbecued Meat

Barbecued Meat is a Manchu dish which has now become a Beijing speciality. In the seventeenth century it was the custom for Qing officials in Beijing to go on picnics in the hills around the capital on the Double Ninth Festival (the ninth day of the ninth month of the lunar calendar). They would bring with them boiled beef or mutton, various seasonings and garnishes, and an iron pan for re-cooking the meat. In some attractive spot they would build a fire, heat the pan over it and sear the cold boiled meat in the pan. The seared meat was then dipped into soy sauce and mashed garlic before being eaten. This dish was gradually introduced into restaurants. About seventy years ago, the recipe was changed to make the meat more palatable: raw beef or mutton was cut into thin slices and marinated before searing. This kind of barbecued meat then became very popular.

It is important to have only choice cuts of meat for this dish. The preparation of mutton for barbecuing is similar to the procedure for Rinsed Mutton described above. The beef comes from a four or five year old animal weighing 150 kilogrammes or more, but only some twenty kilogrammes of meat from the loin and chuck are used. The meat is trimmed and frozen before being cut into strips 16 cm long and 4 cm wide, which are then cut across the grain into three slices. The meat is marinated in a mixture of soy sauce, crushed ginger, wine, shrimp paste, sesame seed paste, rice vinegar and chopped coriander. The meat slices are then seared over high heat on a special barbecue grill 66 cm in diameter. The meat is very tender and has a unique flavour and aroma.

There are two famous Barbecued Meat restaurants in Beijing. The Kaorouji (Barbecued Meat Quarter), which opened in 1848, is picturesquely situated on the banks of the Shishahai (Lake of Ten Monasteries) north of Beihai Park just inside Di'anmen. It is also known for its fried lambs' tails, fried Gansu duck and mutton or prawn shashlik. The Mufeng Barbecued Meat Restaurant, formerly known as the Kaorouyuan (Barbecued Meat Garden), is located near Xuanwumen in the south-western part of the city (the Muslim centre of Beijing) and is over a century old.

Clay-Pot Casseroles

The clay-pot has long been used for cooking in China. Made of earthenware, it is becoming increasingly popular nowadays with families that believe aluminium pots might harm their health. The best pots come from Yixing in Jiangsu and Shiwan in Guangdong.

Apart from home use, the clay-pot is used for making casseroles in many Beijing restaurants. The best-known of these is the Shaguoju (Clay-pots House) Restaurant on South Xisi Street, formerly known as the Heshunju (Harmony House). This restaurant used to be a watch-house during the Qing dynasty. Whole pigs used in sacrificial ceremonies were distributed among the nightwatch-men. Since they could not eat all of the meat them-selves, they set up a restaurant with the leftovers. For over two centuries this restaurant has been using huge clay-pots to turn out wide variety of dishes by stew-ing, frying and simmering. The pork is first simmered in a large clay-pot until it is tender. It is then cubed or sliced, and put into smaller pots with seasonings and other ingredients and cooked over a low heat until it is ready to serve. Among the Shaguoju's best dishes are a cold platter of seasoned pork, called *bairoupian* (white sliced pork), and a soup with sliced pork sausage, called *xuechang* (blood sausage).

14

Appendices

Travel Services

Name	Address	Telephone	Cable	Services
China International Travel Service	6 East Chang'an Avenue	55.1031	LUXINGSHE BEIJING	Travel arrangements and tourist services for foreign groups and individuals in China.
China International Travel Service, Beijing Branch	2 Wang-fujing Street	55.3509	5861	Travel arrangements and tourist services for foreign travellers in the Beijing area and nearby areas such as Tianjin, Taiyuan, Datong and Shijiazhuang.
China Travel Service, Beijing	2 East Qianmen Street	75.7181 ex 708	9499	Travel arrangements in the Beijing area for Chinese compatriots from Xianggang (Hongkong), Aomen (Macao) and Taiwan and overseas Chinese.
Overseas Chinese Travel Service, Beijing Branch	2 Wang-fujing Street	55.4879		Travel arrangements for overseas Chinese returning to China.

Transportation

Taxis	The Capital Car Company offers all kinds of round-the-clock taxi services. Telephone: 55.7461 The Beijing Taxi Company provides buses, stationwagons, taxis and passenger three-wheeled vehicles, and offers round-the-clock service. Telephone: Buses 55.2287 Taxis 55.7661 Three-wheeled Vehicles 55.5661 Qianmen Taxi Station 33.2077 Western District Taxi Station 66.0961 Niujie Street Taxi Station 33.4996 Dongsi Street Taxi Station 44.1056
Railways	Beijing is one of China's major railway junctions connecting with all provincial capitals on the mainland except Lhasa.
Civil Aviation	Beijing is the operations centre of the Civil Aviation Administration of China (CAAC). Scheduled domestic flights are available to all major cities in China, and international flights with connections to Asia, Africa, Europe and North America. CAAC currently provides weekly non-stop flights on the following routes: Beijing — Pyongyang Beijing — Kunming — Rangoon Beijing — Shanghai — Osaka Beijing — Shanghai — Tokyo Beijing — Shanghai — Nagasaki Beijing — Karachi — Paris (Freight) Beijing — Karachi — Addis Ababa

Transportation (continued)

Civil Aviation	

Beijing — Karachi — Belgrade — Zurich
Beijing — Karachi — Bucharest
Beijing — Shanghai — San Francisco — New York
Beijing — Shanghai — San Francisco
Beijing — Sharjah — Paris
Beijing — Sharjah — Frankfort — London
Beijing — Guangzhou — Manila
Beijing — Guangzhou — Bangkok
Beijing — Moscow

There are also three flights a week to Hongkong. Foreign airlines currently provide weekly non-stop flights on the following routes:

Pyongyang — Beijing (Korean Airlines)
Tokyo — Beijing (Japan Air Lines)
Tokyo — Osaka — Shanghai — Beijing (Japan Air Lines)
Paris — Aden — Karachi — Beijing (Air France)
Karachi — Rawalpindi — Beijing — Tokyo (Pakistan Int. Airlines)
Addis Ababa — Bombay — Beijing (Ethiopian Airlines)
Teheran — Beijing — Tokyo (Iran Air)
Zurich — Geneva — Aden — Bombay — Beijing (Swissair)
Bucharest — Karachi — Beijing (Romanian Airlines)
London — Aden — Bombay — Hongkong — Beijing (British Airways)
Belgrade — Dubai — Beijing (Yugoslav Airlines)
Frankfurt — Delhi — Beijing (Lufthausa)
New York — San Francisco — Tokyo — Beijing (PanAm)
Bangkok — Guangzhou (Thai Airways International)
Manila — Guangzhou — Beijing (Philippine Airlines)

Banks

The Bank of China is the state bank for foreign exchange. It has branches in all China's large and medium-sized cities, as well as in Hongkong, London and Singapore. It also has established business–commission relations with over 700 foreign banks in more than 2,000 branches over the world. The following services are available at the Bank of China:

- Buying and selling traveller's checks in Renminbi (Chinese currency);
- Buying and selling foreign currencies in Renminbi;
- Buying and selling traveller's checks in foreign currency;
- Negotiating letters of credit in Renminbi and foreign currency;
- Transferring remittances from abroad by telegraph, mail and bank drafts;
- Collecting foreign currencies and money orders;
- Handling deposits in foreign currency, special deposits in Renminbi and other business concerning foreign exchange.

In addition, the Bank of China has authorized local bank offices and other appointed agents in China to accept traveller's checks in Renminbi. In Beijing these include:

- Bank of China, Business Department of the General Administration Office;
- Bank of China, Dong'anmen Office;
- People's Bank, Liulichang Street Savings Bank;

- Exchange counters at the Beijing Hotel, Friendship Hotel, Nationalities Hotel, Xinqiao Hotel, Qianmen Hotel, Yanjing Hotel, Overseas Chinese Mansion and Overseas Chinese Hotel;
- Exchange counters at the Friendship Store, Capital Airport and the Beijing Arts and Crafts Shop.

Telecommunications and Postal Services

Name	Address	Services	Branches
Beijing Long-distance Tele-communica-tions Bureau	West Chang'an Avenue	International and domestic public telephones and telegrams; international \ and domestic photo-telegrams and domestic facsimile telegrams; international and domestic telex and public telex; rental of special circuit cables for international and inland telex and telephone; relaying of international and domestic broadcasts; relaying of TV programmes via international communications satellite and microwave.	

Telecommunications and Postal Services (continued)

Name	Address	Services	Branches
Beijing Municipal Post and Telecommunications Bureau		International and domestic postal and other services including letter post, parcels, remittances, subscriptions to and retail sale of newspapers, cables, long-distance telephone calls and public telephones.	Post and telecommunications bureaus or stations in Dongsi, Xisi, Wangfujing Street, Di'anmen Street, West Chang'an Avenue, Beixinqiao, Xinjiekou, Beijing Railway Station, Yongdingmen Railway Station and Capital Airport; telecommunications and post offices in the Beijing, Nationalities, Xinqiao and Friendship hotels.
International Postal and Telecommunications Service, Business Section	23 North Dongdan Street, Beijing	Posting international parcels, small packets and printed matter.	
Sales Department of Newspapers and Magazines in Foreign Languages	Wangfujing Street	Selling newspapers and magazines in foreign languages.	

Beijing Temperature Chart (Centigrade)

Month	Max.	Min.	Average	Month	Max.	Min.	Average
January	10.7	−22.8	−4.8	July	39.6	16.1	25.8
February	15.5	−17.6	−2.0	August	38.3	12.3	24.5
March	22.6	−12.5	4.3	September	32.3	4.9	19.5
April	31.1	−2.4	13.3	October	29.3	−1.4	12.6
May	36.6	3.7	19.9	November	23.3	−11.6	4.0
June	38.9	11.2	24.1	December	13.5	−18.0	−2.5

A Brief Chronology of Chinese Historical Periods

Dynasty	Period	Dynasty	Period
Xia dynasty	c. 2100 BC - 1600 BC	Northern and Southern dynasties	420 - 589
Shang dynasty	c. 1600 BC - 1100 BC	Sui dynasty	581 - 618
Western Zhou dynasty	c. 1100 BC - 770 BC	Tang dynasty	618 - 907
Eastern Zhou dynasty	770 BC - 221 BC	Five dynasties	907 - 979
Spring and Autumn period	770 BC - 476 BC	Song dynasty (Northern Song and Southern Song)	960 - 1279
Warring States period	475 BC - 221 BC		
Qin dynasty	221 BC - 207 BC	Liao dynasty	916 - 1125
Western Han dynasty	206 BC - AD 24	Xi Xia dynasty	1038 - 1227
Eastern Han dynasty	25 - 220	Jin dynasty	1115 - 1234
Three Kingdoms period (Wei, Shu, Wu)	220 - 265	Yuan dynasty	1271 - 1368
Western Jin dynasty	265 - 316	Ming dynasty	1368 - 1644
Eastern Jin dynasty	317 - 420	Qing dynasty	1644 - 1911

Chronology of the Ming and Qing Dynasties

Ming (1368-1644)

Dynastic Title (dihao)		Name		Reign Title (nianhao)		Period
Taizu	太祖	Zhu Yuanzhang	朱元璋	Hongwu	洪武	1368 - 1398
Huidi	惠帝	Zhu Yunwen	朱允炆	Jianwen	建文	1399 - 1402
Chengzu	成祖	Zhu Di	朱棣	Yongle	永乐	1403 - 1424
Renzong	仁宗	Zhu Gaochi	朱高炽	Hongxi	洪熙	1425
Xuanzong	宣宗	Zhu Zhanji	朱瞻基	Xuande	宣德	1426 - 1435
Yingzong	英宗	Zhu Qizhen	朱祁镇	Zhengtong	正统	1436 - 1449
Daizong	代宗	Zhu Qiyu	朱祁钰	Jingtai	景泰	1450 - 1456
Yingzong [resumed government]	英宗	Zhu Qizhen	朱祁镇	Tianshun	天顺	1457 - 1464
Xianzong	宪宗	Zhu Jianshen	朱见深	Chenghua	成化	1465 - 1487
Xiaozong	孝宗	Zhu Youcheng	朱祐樘	Hongzhi	弘治	1488 - 1505
Wuzong	武宗	Zhu Houzhao	朱厚照	Zhengde	正德	1506 - 1521
Shizong	世宗	Zhu Houcong	朱厚熜	Jiajing	嘉靖	1522 - 1566
Muzong	穆宗	Zhu Zaihou	朱载垕	Longqing	隆庆	1567 - 1572
Shenzong	神宗	Zhu Yijun	朱翊钧	Wanli	万历	1573 - 1620
Guangzong	光宗	Zhu Changluo	朱常洛	Taichang	泰昌	1620 (29 days)
Xizong	熹宗	Zhu Youxiao	朱由校	Tianqi	天启	1621 - 1627
Sizong	思宗	Zhu Youjian	朱由检	Chongzhen	崇祯	1628 - 1644

Qing (1644-1911)

Dynastic Title (dihao)		Name	Reign Title (nianhao)		Period
Taizu	太祖	Aisin-Gioro Nurhachi 爱新觉罗努尔哈赤	Tianming	天命	1616 - 1626
Taizong	太宗	Aisin-Gioro Huang Taiji 皇太极	Tiancong	天聪	1627 - 1635
			Chongde	崇德	1636 - 1643
Shizu	世祖	Aisin-Gioro Fulin 福临	Shunzhi	顺治	1644 - 1661
Shengzu	圣祖	Aisin-Gioro Xuanye 玄烨	Kangxi	康熙	1662 - 1722
Shizong	世宗	Aisin-Gioro Yinzhen 胤禛	Yongzheng	雍正	1723 - 1735
Gaozong	高宗	Aisin-Gioro Hongli 弘历	Qianlong	乾隆	1736 - 1795
Renzong	仁宗	Aisin-Gioro Yongyan 颙琰	Jiaqing	嘉庆	1796 - 1820
Xuanzong	宣宗	Aisin-Gioro Minning 旻宁	Daoguang	道光	1821 - 1850
Wenzong	文宗	Aisin-Gioro Yizhu 奕詝	Xianfeng	咸丰	1851 - 1861
Muzong	穆宗	Aisin-Gioro Zaichun 载淳	Tongzhi	同治	1862 - 1874
Dezong	德宗	Aisin-Gioro Zaitian 载湉	Guangxu	光绪	1875 - 1908
[no dynastic title]		Aisin-Gioro Puyi 溥仪	Xuantong	宣统	1909 - 1911

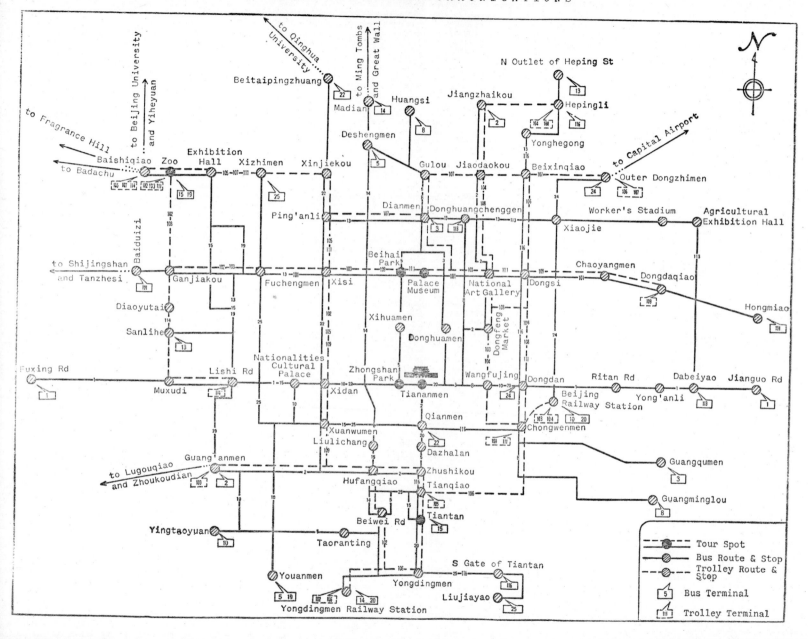

BEIJING URBAN COMMUNICATIONS

北　京

刘俊雯　编

*

外文出版社出版
（中国北京百万庄路24号）
邮政编码100037
北京外文印刷厂印刷
中国国际图书贸易总公司发行
（中国北京车公庄西路21号）
北京邮政信箱第399号　邮政编码100044
1982年（32开）第一版
1991年第二版
（英）
ISBN 7-119-01221-5/K·70（外）
01155
12——E——1585P

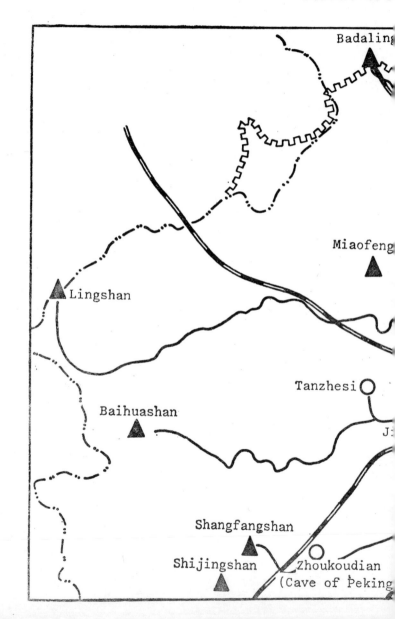

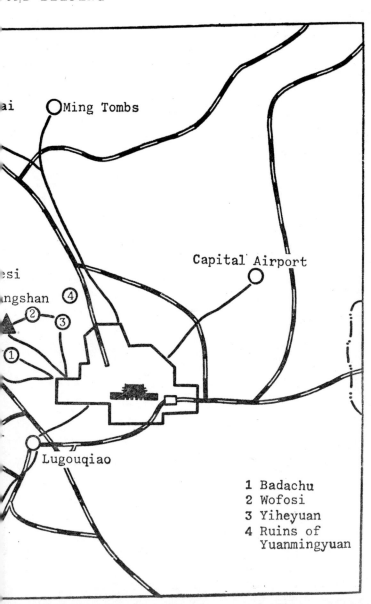

1 Badachu
2 Wofosi
3 Yiheyuan
4 Ruins of
  Yuanmingyuan